ribeya

A ROOM FOR TWO

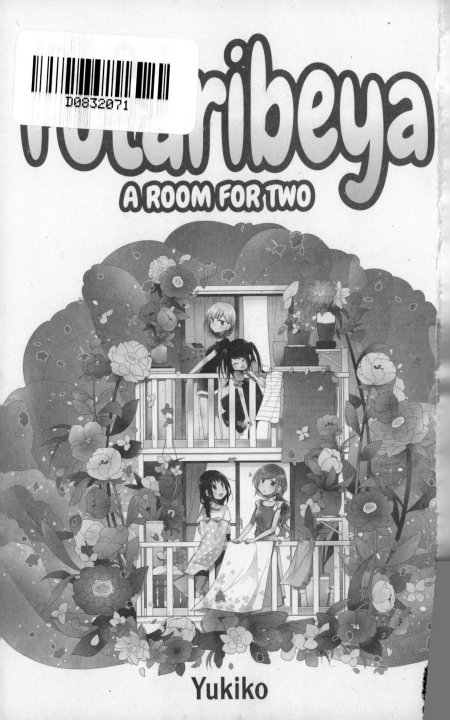

Yukiko

Contents

SAKURAKO AND KASUMI BECAME CLOSE FRIENDS WHEN THEY MOVED INTO THE BOARDING HOUSE TOGETHER AFTER STARTING HIGH SCHOOL. THEY'RE SECOND YEARS NOW, AND HAVING FUN EVERY DAY WITH THEIR NEW UNDERCLASSMEN FRIENDS!

KASUMI YAMABUKI
A BEAUTIFUL BUT OVERLY RELAXED AND LAZY ONLY CHILD WHO FOLLOWS HER OWN CONVICTIONS. BIG EATER.
SAKURAKO KAWAWA
TOP OF THE CLASS. HAS THE TEMPERAMENT OF AN OLDER SISTER AND IS GOOD AT COOKING AND CLEANING. HAS AN OLDER SISTER, YOUNGER BROTHER, AND YOUNGER SISTER.
SHOUKO AKASHI
A FIRST YEAR ROOMING WITH SERI. SHE'S A MEMBER OF THE TRACK TEAM AND HAS A FRANK AND STRONG-MINDED PERSONALITY. EVERYONE CALLS HER SHOUKO.
SERI FURUYASHIKI
A FIRST-YEAR ROOMING WITH SHOUKO. SHE'S A SHELTERED RICH GIRL WHO USES OVERLY POLITE SPEECH WITH EVERYONE SHE MEETS.
STORY
and
CHARACTERS

Chapter 23

WE SHOULD HAVE HOTPOT TOGETHER!

EVERYONE BRINGS ONE OR TWO INGREDIENTS!
SO...

*KASUMI'S AT WORK.
I'LL BUY SOMETHING ON MY WAY HOME.
HMM...
I CAN'T THINK OF ANYTHING.
I GUESS I'LL BRAIN-STORM IDEAS AT THE STORE.

HMM...
I DON'T WANT TO PUT ANYTHING TOO WEIRD IN...
SEAWEED
SALE

WHOOPS!
I COULDN'T DECIDE, SO I ENDED UP BUYING TOO MUCH!
CORNFLAKES

ガチャ
KER-CHAK
THANKS FOR HAVING US OVER!

NO PROBLEM!
TO START, I MADE SOUP FOR THE HOTPOT!

WE KNEW YOU'D BE ON TOP OF THINGS.
THANKS, SAKU-RAKO.

HEY, AZUSA, WHAT'S IN THAT BAG?
IT LOOKS SUSPICIOUS.
IT'S A SECRET!

I'LL TURN OFF THE LIGHTS.
OKAY!

パチンッ
FLICK
EVERYONE, PUT IN YOUR INGREDI- ENTS!
HEHE! I CAN'T SEE ANYTHING!
JUST BE CAREFUL!

ゴッ
CLANG
ゴッ
CLANG
チャポ…
CRACK
ポチャン
KERPLUNK
ゴンッ
CLANG
ボチャボチャ
DRIP
DRIP
ゴンッ
CLANG
ゴトッ
KATHUNK

THAT SOUNDED OMINOUS...
IT'S EDIBLE, RIGHT?
WHO WAS THAT?

YOU HAVE TO EAT WHAT YOU PICK UP!
READY?
WAH, THIS IS SO SCARY!

OH, IS THIS A GYOZA?
I CAN JUST BARELY SEE IT
SO LUCKY!

パク
CHOMP
UGH!

IT'S SWEET!
AND MUSHY...
IT'S FULL OF WHIPPED CREAM!
I MADE THEM MYSELF!
GROSS...

MINE IS KIND OF... HEAVY.
CAN YOU TURN THE LIGHT ON?
SURE.

FLICK
パチッ
A CUCUMBER?!
SO THAT'S WHAT MADE THE THUNKING NOISE.

GEEZ!
AT LEAST CUT IT UP FIRST!
WHY PUT IT IN WHOLE?
CHOMP
パクッ

I-IS IT GOOD?
ボリッ
CRUNCH
ボリッ
CRUNCH
NOT BAD, ACTUALLY.

I PUT KONJAC JELLY IN, BUT IT MELTED...
I CAN'T SEE IT.
WHAT CRAZY INGREDIENTS...

I'M SO FULL!
I COULD EAT MORE...

?!
ポヨーン
BOUNCE

IT'S ALL STUCK TOGETH-ER!
I TOOK THE ENTIRE THING OUT!
!
IS THAT BECAUSE OF THE JELLY?
JIGGLE
プルプル
JIGGLE

BY THE WAY...
KASUMI, WHAT DID YOU PUT IN?

CHICKEN WINGS, PORK SLICES, AND CHICKEN MEATBALLS.
PHEW...
I ATE SO MUCH.

ALL YOUR INGREDI-ENTS WERE NORMAL.
BUT THEY WERE ALL MEAT...

WELL, YOU DON'T USUALLY PUT THAT MUCH MEAT INTO HOTPOTS.
YEAH, BUT...
IF I'M GOING TO EAT...
I WANT TO EAT SOMETHING DELICIOUS.

THE NEXT DAY...

I WANT TO HAVE HOTPOT AGAIN.

AS LONG AS WE DON'T HAVE TO EAT IN THE DARK!

THEN HOW ABOUT KIMCHI WITH SOY MILK SOUP AND CHEESE?

WHY DO YOU ALWAYS WANT TO MIX UP THE FLAVORS?

TIMETABLE

OUR HISTORY CLASS IS GOING TO BE HELD IN THE AV ROOM!

OKAY!

THIS IS OUR FIRST TIME COMING TO THE AV ROOM.
IT'S PRETTY BIG!

WHAT'S WRONG, KASUMI?
AREN'T YOU GOING TO SIT DOWN?
カチッ
CLACK

キョロ
GLANCE

I BOUGHT AN ELECTRIC BLANKET!
AH...
ARE YOU GETTING READY TO NAP?!
YOU EVEN HAVE A PILLOW!
ぽかぽか
WARM WARM

WHEN THE EVENT OCCURRED, THE PEOPLE WERE...
ZZZ...
ZZZ...

THIS CONCLUDES OUR CLASS FOR TODAY.
PLEASE WRITE A REPORT ON YOUR THOUGHTS AND HAND IT IN NEXT TIME.
YES, MA'AM.
YAY, WHAT AN EASY CLASS!

KASUMI, WILL YOU BE ABLE TO WRITE THE REPORT?
WERE YOU EVEN WATCHING?
HNGH...

WE DON'T HAVE TO TAKE OUT THE TRASH TODAY... LET ME SLEEP 5 MORE MINUTES...
MUMBLE むにゃ
MUMBLE むにゃ
HEY!
WE'RE AT SCHOOL!

I FELL ASLEEP, SO CAN I WATCH IT AGAIN?
I'M SORRY.
SURE, GO AHEAD.
I'M GOING BACK TO THE TEACHERS' LOUNGE, SO CLEAN UP WHEN YOU'RE DONE.

HMM?
DVD

HEY!
DID SHE SAY IT WAS OKAY?
I'LL WATCH IT WITH YOU, IF YOU WANT.

I FOUND A HORROR MOVIE!
WHAT?!
DVD
CURSED HOSPITAL AT MIDNIGHT

THIS JUST CAME OUT ON DVD! LET'S WATCH IT!
IT WAS IN THE DRAWER.

I'LL GO PUT IT IN.
YOU'RE REALLY GOING TO WATCH IT?
WH-WHAT?
WHAT ABOUT THE DVD FOR CLASS?

IF YOU'RE SCARED, YOU CAN GO BACK TO THE CLASSROOM.
YOU DON'T HAVE TO STAY.
I'LL WATCH THE ONE FOR CLASS LATER.

I DON'T WANT TO GO BACK ALONE, EITHER...
UH, UM...
I'M HITTING PLAY!
OKAY!
WHIMPER
あうあう
WHIMPER

CRASH
WAAAH!

IT WASN'T THAT GOOD, WAS IT?
JUST FULL OF JUMP SCARES.
AND NOT VERY ORIGINAL...

SAKURAKO, ARE YOU STILL ALIVE?
...3689 1254...
MUMBLE MUMBLE
PAT

COUNTING OUT PI REALLY HELPED!
SAKURAKO, YOU'RE WHAT'S SCARY.
ハア
HUFF
ハア
HUFF
I DON'T REMEMBER ANYTHING FROM THE MOVIE, THOUGH.

WHY DO PEOPLE AROUND THE WORLD ENJOY HORROR MOVIES?
I DON'T GET IT...
はぁぁ...
SIGH

HMM...
MAYBE BECAUSE THEY GET A THRILL FROM SEEING SCARY THINGS?

IF THAT'S ALL THEY WANT, THEY COULD JUST LOOK UNDER A ROCK IN A FIELD SOME-WHERE!
CANNOT BE SHOWN!
NO ONE WANTS TO SEE THAT.
WAAAH

IF THEY WANTED A THRILL THEY COULD GO BUNGEE JUMPING WITHOUT THE ROPE!
THEY'D JUST DIE.
ARE YOU CRAZY?

BUT RECENTLY I HAVEN'T BEEN THAT SCARED...
OF HORROR MOVIES.

REALLY? WHY NOT?
YOU LOOK SCARED TO ME.

BECAUSE I HAVE SOMEONE WHO IS ALWAYS WITH ME! ♡
ぎゅっ
SQUEEZE

I'M FINE WHEN I STICK TO SOMEONE WHO ISN'T SCARED!
IN THE END, YOU'RE STILL SCARED IF YOU'RE BY YOURSELF.
PLUS YOU'RE HEAVY...

HEY...
THERE ARE OTHER HORROR MOVIES HERE!
WE HAVE STUDY HALL NEXT PERIOD, SO WE CAN WATCH THEM!

I HEARD THIS ONE IS SUPER SCARY!
IT GOT GREAT REVIEWS.
I GUESS THE JAPANESE HISTORY TEACHER LIKES HORROR.

SHRIEK
YOU'RE FINE AS LONG AS YOU STICK TO ME, RIGHT?

YOU SHOULD JUST GO BACK TO THE CLASSROOM AT THIS POINT.
I CAN'T S-SEE...
YOU'VE HAD ENOUGH.

MY SWEATER'S ALL STRETCHED OUT...

SORRY.

Illustration gallery of Yukiko

Futaribeya
A ROOM FOR TWO

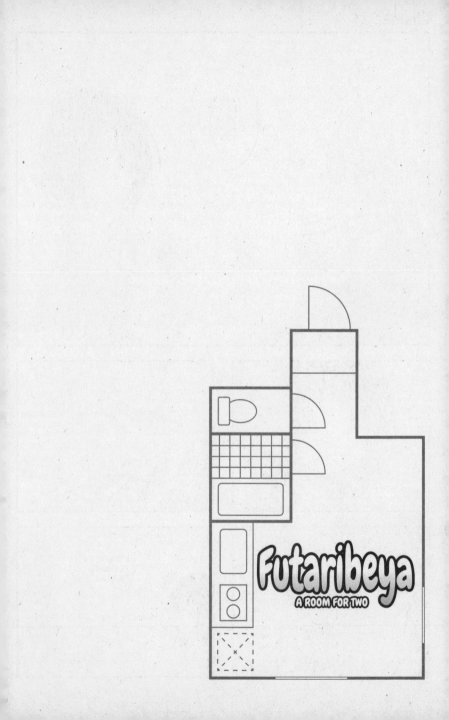

Chapter 24

BY THE WAY...
WHAT ARE YOU GOING TO DO FOR NEW YEAR'S?
12 December

HMM...
MY MOM KEEPS TELLING ME TO COME HOME, BUT...
STRETCH
によーん

I DON'T REALLY FEEL LIKE GOING HOME, EITHER.
I'LL JUST GO TO WISH THEM A HAPPY NEW YEAR.

HONESTLY, IT'S JUST A PAIN.
YEAH...

MORE IMPORTANTLY, I'M LOOKING FORWARD TO OUR CHRISTMAS CAKE AND NEW YEAR'S MOCHI SOUP!
I'LL DO MY BEST TO MAKE THEM!

NEW YEAR'S?
I'M GOING HOME.

OH.
YOU'RE NOT GOING TO LEAVE FOR THE BREAK?
HUH? SERI, YOU'RE GOING HOME?

I'M STAYING BEHIND, TOO.
I LIVE PRETTY FAR AWAY.

THEN... YOU SHOULD COME OVER TO OUR ROOM FOR NEW YEAR'S EVE.
WE CAN HAVE HOTPOT.
SOUNDS GREAT!
OH, UM...

ぐでっ
FLOP
RECENTLY I FEEL LIKE I UNDERSTAND HERMIT CRABS BETTER...

HUH? WHY?
HERMIT CRABS?

CRUNCH
ボリ
CRUNCH
ボリ
HERMIT CRABS CARRY THEIR SHELLS ON THEIR BACKS.
YEAH. SO?

I WANT TO GO TO SCHOOL LIKE THIS, TOO.
YOU ALREADY TAKE YOUR BLANKET AND PILLOW WITH YOU...

WHEN I WAS LITTLE, I WAS CALLED SNAIL.
BY MY OLDER SISTER.

WOW...
WHY?
BACK THEN...

I WAS REALLY, REALLY SHY, AND EVERY TIME I MET A STRANGER...
HELLO!
JOLT

I'D RUN AND HIDE BEHIND MY OLDER SISTER.
SISTER
LIKE A SNAIL...
POKE

YOU WERE THE SHY TYPE, HUH?
I DIDN'T EXPECT THAT.

WHAT ABOUT YOU? WHAT WERE YOU LIKE?
HMM...

I WASN'T SHY, BUT I WAS REALLY BAD AT REMEM-BERING PEOPLE'S FACES.

I OFTEN FOLLOWED STRANGERS AROUND THINKING THEY WERE MY MOM
WHO ARE YOU?!
THAT'S SO DANGER-OUS...

AND YOU NEVER GOT KID-NAPPED?
I CAN'T BELIEVE IT...

MY FRIENDS PROTECTED ME...
SO THAT NEVER HAPPENED.

ALMOST AN 8-INCH HEIGHT DIFFERENCE
BUT EVEN THOUGH I WAS WITH KIDS MY OWN AGE...
KASUMI, DON'T WANDER OFF!

PEOPLE THOUGHT I WAS BABY-SITTING THEM.
HAHA!
RATHER THAN BEING KIDNAPPED, I LOOKED LIKE A KIDNAPPER...

AH...
I HAVE TO PREORDER OUR CHRISTMAS CAKE!
ALTHOUGH I COULD JUST MAKE ONE...

DOES THE CAKE SHOP YOU WORK AT ACCEPT ORDERS?
YEAH, THEY DO.
I'LL PLACE AN ORDER.
THEIR CAKE IS ALWAYS DELICIOUS!

GASP
は
THERE'S SOME-THING I'VE ALWAYS WANTED TO DO...
キ
GLINT
WHAT IS IT?

I WANT TO EAT AN ENTIRE CAKE BY MYSELF!
THEN LET'S BUY TWO CAKES THIS YEAR!

CHRISTMAS DAY...
MERRY CHRISTMAS!
CLINK

YAY!
AT LEAST THAT'S WHAT SHOULD HAVE HAPPENED...

I MIGHT FREEZE TO DEATH...
WHY ARE WE OUTSIDE?
TO CATCH PEOPLE ON THEIR WAY HOME.
WHAT ARE YOU EVEN SAYING? YOU'RE STILL YOUNG.
WOULD YOU LIKE TO BUY A CAKE?
SHIVER
SHIVER
SHORTCAKE
800 YEN
YULE LOG
800 YEN

HOW OLD ARE YOU AGAIN?
SHOULD YOU BE WEARING THAT?
IF YOU ASK THAT ONE MORE TIME, I'LL FIRE YOU!

OH, SAKURAKO...

KASUMI, YOU LOOK SO CUTE! TEE-HEE!

YOU DIDN'T COME TO SCHOOL WRAPPED IN A BLANKET TODAY.

WELL, I'VE GOT OTHER COUNTER-MEASURES IN PLACE.

WHEN MY HANDS GET COLD, I WARM THEM ON SAKURAKO'S NECK.
HEY, CUT IT OUT!

① BACK
I'VE GOT A TUMMY WARMER ON, WITH LOTS OF HAND WARMERS.
②
③ BOTTOMS OF HER FEET
④

WHEN WE'RE OUTSIDE, I MAKE SURE I'M DOWNWIND OF HER.
IS THAT REALLY SOMETHING TO LOOK SO PROUD OF?

I'M SORRY
HMPH
GEEZ!
I WON'T WARM YOU UP ANY-MORE!

AH...
GOOD EVENING. I HAD SOMETHING I WANTED TO ASK THE LANDLORD...
WHAT IS IT?
BE BACK IN A BIT!
HMM?
SERI, WHAT'S UP?

IT WASN'T MENTIONED WHEN WE MOVED IN, EITHER, SO I IMAGINED THERE WAS A MISTAKE OF SOME KIND...
OUR FLOOR IS SO COLD, BUT I CANNOT FIND THE SWITCH FOR THE BUILT-IN HEATER...

WHAT?!
I-IS THAT SO?
BUT I REALLY WANT ONE...
MOST APART-MENTS DON'T COME WITH FLOOR HEATERS.

SENSITIVITY?
KASUMI, YOUR SENSITIVITY TO THE HEAT AND THE COLD IS TOO EXTREME.

SAKURAKO WEARS THE SAME CLOTHES ALL YEAR ROUND. THAT'S PRETTY AMAZING, TOO.

NO...
IT'S STRANGE. AFTER ALL...
HUH?
I THINK IT'S NORMAL.

I'M NOT!
MAYBE SHE'S A ROBOT.
ARE YOU COLD-BLOODED OR SOMETHING?
YOU RARELY SWEAT IN SUMMER, AND IN THE WINTER YOU CAN WALK AROUND IN SHORT SLEEVES FOR AN HOUR AFTER GETTING OUT OF THE SHOWER.

*KAGAMI MOCHI IS A NEW YEAR'S DECORATION MADE OF TWO RICE CAKES STACKED ON EACH OTHER AND TOPPED WITH AN ORANGE.

*OSECHI IS FOOD PREPARED IN SPECIAL BOXES BEFORE NEW YEAR'S SO THAT FAMILIES DON'T HAVE TO COOK OVER THE HOLIDAY.

DING ピン
DONG ポーン
HMM? WHO COULD THAT BE?

I'LL GET IT!
THANKS.

KER-CHAK ガチャッ
UM...
MAY I CELEBRATE NEW YEAR'S WITH YOU ALL?

SORRY TO INTRUDE.
OH, WELCOME BACK!

THE COUNTDOWN IS STARTING SOON!

AHHH, I CAN'T EAT ANY MORE!

Illustration gallery of Yukiko

Futaribeya
A ROOM FOR TWO

Chapter 25

JANUARY 1ST

KASUMI, LET'S VISIT A SHRINE THIS YEAR!

SPLASH

WE CAN JUST GO TO THE SMALL SHRINE IN OUR NEIGHBOR-HOOD!
WHY...
DO YOU WANT TO GO SO BADLY?

I GUESS I HAVE NO CHOICE.
BUT IT'S SO COLD...

モコ
FLUFFY
モッコ
FLUFFY
モコ
FLUFFY

SHOULD I GIVE YOU ANOTHER SCARF?
ぐるっ
WRAP
モゴ
FLUFFY
I CAN'T BREATHE...
モゴ
FLUFFY

パン
CLAP
パン
CLAP

WHAT DID YOU WISH FOR?
I PRAYED THAT WE COULD BE TOGETHER FOREVER!

UM...
SHOULD I BE HONEST?
I PRAYED THAT I'LL ALWAYS BE ABLE TO EAT...

YOUR FOOD...
WOW! I'LL DO MY BEST TO COOK FOR YOU!

LET'S GET OUR FORTUNES TOLD!
NO THANKS.
RATTLE ガラ
RATTLE ガラ
FORTUNES

FORTUNES
#28
GREAT MISFORTUNE
OH NO! I GOT THE WORST LUCK!

DOES SOMETHING HAPPEN IF YOU DRAW GREAT MIS-FORTUNE?
HUH?

IT'S ALL I'VE EVER RECEIVED BEFORE, BUT NOTH-ING REALLY HAP-PENED...
THAT'S WHY I DON'T GET MY FORTUNE TOLD ANYMORE.
IT'S THE PRINCIPLE OF THE THING.

AH!...
MISS NATSUKI!
HEY, YOU TWO!

WE'RE MAKING MOCHI!
IN THE COURTYARD!
YAY!
わい CHEER
わい CHEER

WHY DON'T YOU JUST BUY THE KIND THAT'S ALREADY MADE?
THAT LOOKS LIKE WORK...

YOU'RE NO FUN, KASUMI.
PLUS FRESH MOCHI TASTES BETTER!
BUT IT TAKES SO MUCH EFFORT...
THE PRE-PACKAGED KIND IS GOOD TOO, YOU KNOW.

KASUMI, POUND THE MOCHI!
ドキドキ
BA-DUMP
GO FOR IT!
UGH...

ALL READY! GO AHEAD!

ぺちっ
SMACK
ぺちっ
SMACK

MY ARMS ARE ALREADY TIRED...
へろ
PLUNK
HEY!
IT'LL NEVER BE READY, AT THIS RATE!

I'LL DO IT!
I-
I'LL TRY, TOO!
THANKS.

OKAY...
HERE GOES!
ALL RIGHT!
わく
EXCITED
わく
EXCITED

ゴ
WHAM
ドッ
POUND

ヒッ
EEK
N-NO WAY... THAT'S SO SCARY...
HUH?
SHOUKO, RESTRAIN YOURSELF...

FRESH MOCHI IS SO GOOD!
OM
NOM
NICE AND SOFT!

WHEN IT'S THIS SOFT, I'M NOT SURE HOW MUCH I SHOULD CHEW IT.
I FEEL LIKE I COULD SWALLOW IT WHOLE.
CHEW PROPERLY, PLEASE.
IT'LL GET STUCK IN YOUR THROAT.
SQUISH
SQUISH

STRETCH
CHEW
CHEW
CHEW
CHEW
CHEW
CHEW
CHEW

HOW LONG HAS SHE BEEN CHEWING THAT ONE PIECE?
WHEN IS SHE GOING TO SWALLOW?
CHEW
CHEW
CHEW
CHEW
CHEW
CHEW

YEAH!

RED BEAN SOUP IS DELICIOUS TOO!

Illustration gallery of Yukiko

WINTER SETTING
KASUMI'S SKIRT IS SHORT BECAUSE SHE DOESN'T OWN A WINTER UNIFORM, SO SHE'S WEARING HER SUMMER SKIRT.

Chapter 26

IT'S VALENTINE'S DAY.

SO HEAVY...

WOW!

I'M GOING TO CRAM SCHOOL NOW.
I JUST STARTED GOING RECENTLY.
OKAY! SEE YOU LATER!

FRESH FROM THE SHOWER! ♪
KER-CHAK
I'M HOME.

WELCOME BA—

YOU GOT EVEN MORE CHOCO-LATE!
SO HEAVY... MY ARMS ARE GOING TO BREAK...
I'M HAPPY, THOUGH.

THAT SATURDAY...
IT'S A LITTLE LATE, BUT HAPPY VALENTINE'S DAY! ♡

SINCE YOU'RE GETTING READY FOR EXAMS, YOU SHOULD FOCUS ON STUDYING, NOT CHOCOLATE!
IT'S A PEN...
I HEARD THAT SHE ALWAYS RECEIVES A LOT, SO I BOUGHT STATIONERY INSTEAD! ♡

BESIDES, DIDN'T YOU GIVE HER CHOCOLATE TOO?
I JUST WANTED TO GIVE HER SOMETHING MYSELF!

THIS YEAR SHE GAVE IT TO ME, INSTEAD.
SO I'LL GIVE HER SOMETHING ON WHITE DAY*.
WHAT?!
THAT'S NO FAIR!
PROUD

*WHITE DAY, MARCH 14TH, IS WHEN THE PEOPLE WHO RECEIVED CHOCOLATES ON VALENTINE'S DAY RETURN THE FAVOR.

I'M GLAD I RECEIVED SO MUCH CHOCO-LATE.
I GUESS I SHOULD HAVE GONE WITH CHOCOLATE AFTER ALL...
REALLY?

SINCE I STARTED GOING TO CRAM SCHOOL I'VE HAD TO CUT BACK ON MY WORK SHIFTS,
SO I DON'T HAVE AS MUCH FOOD MONEY.

NOW I WON'T HAVE TO BUY DESSERT.

BUT AT CRAM SCHOOL THE ENTIRE ROOM SMELLED LIKE CHOCOLATE AND ALL THE BOYS WERE GLARING AT ME.
THEY SAID, "SOMEONE'S STILL EATING CHOCOLATE?"
WOW...
POOR KASUMI.

I HAVE PLANS TOMORROW, SO I'LL GO HOME NOW.
THANKS, SAKU!
BE CAREFUL.
IT'S DARK OUTSIDE.

OH...
HINA.
WAIT.
HUH?

SORRY I COULDN'T GIVE IT TO YOU ON VALENTINE'S DAY, BUT...
HERE YOU GO.

I'LL KEEP IT FOR-EVER!
NO...
PLEASE EAT IT.
SORRY IT'S NOT HANDMADE OR ANYTHING.

*A JAPANESE HOLIDAY MARKING THE END OF WINTER LEADING UP TO THE BEGINNING OF SPRING.
**ON SETSUBUN, BEANS ARE THROWN AT "DEMONS" DRESSED UP IN MASKS TO SIGNIFY THE RELEASE OF BAD OMENS FROM THE HOME AND BRING IN GOOD LUCK.

DO YOU THINK HINA WILL BE ABLE TO GET INTO OUR SCHOOL?
I DON'T THINK SHE'LL HAVE A PROBLEM.
わしゃ WASH
わしゃ WASH

SHE ALWAYS PULLS THROUGH DURING ACTUAL TESTS.
ザバーッ SPLASH
REALLY?
I HAD NO IDEA.
OOF!

ENTRANCE EXAMS, HUH...
ちゃぷ DRIP
...HM?

WHAT?
I CAN'T REMEMBER MINE...
?
IT WAS ONLY TWO YEARS AGO, AND YOU ALREADY FORGOT?!
ARE YOU OKAY?!

TWO YEARS AGO, THE DAY OF THE ACCEPTANCE ANNOUNCEMENT...

ざわ CHATTER
ざわ CHATTER

DID YOU FIND YOUR NUMBER?

I CAN'T REALLY SEE, BUT IT'S PROBABLY UP THERE.

I PASSED! LET'S GO HOME.

WAIL

I'VE GOT A HUGE PIMPLE!

EATING LUNCH IN THE CAFETERIA
SKIN CARE?

I GET DRY SKIN IN WINTER, SO I ALWAYS APPLY MOISTURIZER AFTER I SHOWER!

ME TOO! MY SKIN IS SO DRY...
RIGHT?
YEP!
I...

SOME-TIMES FORGET TO WASH MY FACE.
ESPECIALLY AFTER I WAKE UP.
UGH, THAT MAKES ME WANT TO PUNCH YOU.

SQUEEZE
URGH...
I CAN'T BELIEVE IT'S SO NICE EVEN THOUGH YOU DON'T DO ANY-THING...
GLISTEN

LIFE IS SO UNFAIR!
E-
EVEN IF YOU SAY THAT...
YOU'RE SO HEAVY.

LATER...
I'LL HAVE MY MOM SEND ME SOME OF HER SKIN CARE PRODUCTS FOR TEENS.
SHE RUNS A BEAUTY TREATMENT COURSE.

HUH?
REALLY?
SPARKLE
SO EASY TO PLEASE...

I ALWAYS HAVE SO MANY DIFFERENT KINDS OF LIP BALM.
I CAN'T USE THEM ALL UP.
THAT'S TOO MANY, AZUSA...
CAN I BORROW ONE?
ME TOO.
バラ ROLL
ROLL バラ

IT'S SO RELAXING WHEN YOUR LIP BALM SMELLS NICE, ISN'T IT?
I LIKE JASMINE SCENT!

OH...
THIS ONE TASTES LIKE BANANA.
IT'S NICE.
THIS ONE TASTES LIKE CHOCOLATE!
IT'S SO SWEET!

RECENTLY I'M INTO AROMATHERAPY, SO IF YOU HAVE A FAVORITE SCENT I'LL LEND IT TO YOU!
WHAT SCENTS DO YOU LIKE?
WOW!

IF YOU MIX THEM, YOUR LIPS WILL TASTE LIKE CHOCOLATE-COVERED BANANAS!
HA-HA!

I LIKE DELICIOUS-SMELLING SCENTS!

H-HEY!
WANT TO TRY MIXING THEM?
KASUMI?!
WE'RE AT SCHOOL!
WHAT ARE THEY EVEN DOING?

UM...
LIKE COCONUT OR VANILLA?
うっ
とり
DAZED
MORE LIKE MEAT FLAVORS...
M-
MEAT?!

IT'S BEST TO PUT YOUR TONER ON THE PALM OF YOUR HAND AND PAT IT IN!
...

KASUMI, PUT OUT YOUR HAND.
HMM?
パシャ
SPLASH

?!
ぴと
PAT

WHAT ARE YOU DOING?
I THOUGHT YOUR HANDS WOULD HAVE A BETTER EFFECT THAN MINE!

I HEARD NOT GETTING ENOUGH SLEEP IS BAD FOR YOUR SKIN...
SO I'M GOING TO BED EARLY!
GOOD NIGHT.

I NEED TO REVIEW FOR TOMORROW...

SCRITCH
カリ
SCRITCH
カリ
SCRITCH
カリ...

CAN'T SLEEP?
?
SLITHER
ずず ず...
I CAN'T RELAX WHEN YOU'RE NOT LYING BESIDE ME.

THE NEXT MORNING...
シャコ BRUSH
シャコ BRUSH
YESTERDAY, I WAS THINKING...
ペチ PAT
ペチ PAT
HUH?

AREN'T PIMPLES CAUSED...

BY EATING TOO MUCH CHOCOLATE?
AND YOU HAD A LOT FOR VALENTINE'S DAY...
!

THAT'S IT!
PROBABLY!
ガラ GARGLE
ガラ GARGLE

DOING A FACE MASK...

CAN I TAKE A PIC?

ABSOLUTELY NOT.

Illustration gallery of Yukiko

Futaribeya
A ROOM FOR TWO

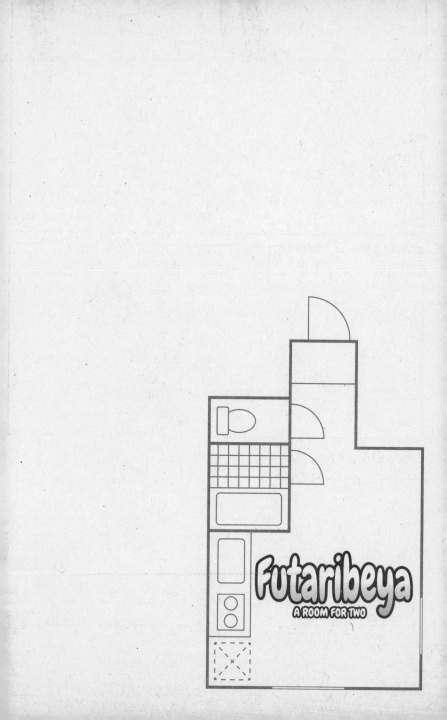

MESTER
RADES

THIRD YEAR CLASS #2 STUDENT NUMBER 7 (HINAKO KAWAWA)

UGH...

Special Chapter #1 - "A Day in Hinako's Life"

I WONDER IF I'LL DO WELL ON MY EXAMS...

THE TRAIN IS ARRIVING ON TRACK 3.

BEEP

IT TAKES ALMOST TWO HOURS BY TRAIN TO GET FROM OUR HOUSE...

TO SAKU'S BOARDING HOUSE.

11:32
SATURDAY

AT LEAST THERE AREN'T MANY TRANS-FERS.

BUT I'M SO SLEEPY...

YAWN

MY NAME IS HINAKO KAWAWA, AND I'M IN MY LAST YEAR OF MIDDLE SCHOOL.

MY OLDER SISTER, SAKURAKO, TUTORS ME AT HER BOARDING HOUSE ON THE WEEKENDS.

CLICKETY-CLACK

THE NEXT STATION IS... ZAWA.

CLICKETY-CLACK

ZZZ...

GASP

OH NO!

DID I RIDE PAST MY STOP?!

I HAVE TO GET OFF!

DASH

プシュー
WHOOSH
ッ

WHERE... AM I?
タタン
CLICKETY-CLACK
タタン
CLICKETY-CLACK
I GOT OFF THE TRAIN WITHOUT CHECKING...
キョロ
GLANCE

OH, I'LL USE MY PHONE.
RUSTLE
ゴソ
YOU'VE GOT TO BE KIDDING ME.
SERIOUSLY?
OUT OF JUICE...

OH, I'M NOT ACTUALLY THAT FAR.
PHEW
ほっ

I ALWAYS EAT LUNCH AT SAKU'S HOUSE...
BUT I GUESS I'LL EAT HERE.
ぐう
GURGLE

WacDon

CHOMP
もぐ
CHOMP
MAYBE I SHOULD BUY SOMETHING SMALL TO TAKE WITH ME.
SOMETHING SWEET?
NOT TOO LONG AGO...
KASUMI ATE AN ENTIRE CAKE BY HERSELF.
NOT THAT I CARED.
IT WAS FINE.
I COULD HAVE EATEN MORE.
KASUMI...

SHE'S SO GORGEOUS AND HAS A GREAT FIGURE...
BUT I'M ALWAYS SO AMAZED BY HOW MUCH SHE CAN EAT!
REFILL
I ALWAYS GAIN WEIGHT WHEN I EAT WITH YOU!
CAN YOU PLEASE SLOW DOWN?
YOU MAKE ME WANT TO EAT MORE TOO!
THAT'S NOT MY FAULT...
CHUCKLE
THREE CREAM PUFFS, PLEASE.

COME AGAIN!
PUFFS
I HOPE THEY LIKE CREAM PUFFS!

SAKU IS TWO YEARS OLDER THAN ME.

SHE'S EXTREMELY TALENTED AND HAS HER HEAD ON STRAIGHT.
EVERYONE IN OUR FAMILY IS PROUD OF HER.

SHE ALWAYS DECIDES THINGS BY HER-SELF...
SO SHE'S NEVER ASKED ME FOR ADVICE ON ANYTHING.

I NEVER THOUGHT SHE'D DECIDE TO STAY IN A BOARDING HOUSE AT A SCHOOL FAR AWAY.

BUT WHEN I WENT TO VISIT HER, I REALIZED THAT SHE WAS HAVING A GREAT TIME WITH HER ROOMMATE, KASUMI.
SHOCK
呆

HMPH

OH, THAT HAIR TIE IS CUTE!
SALE
SALE

IT'S LIGHT BLUE AND SUPER FLUFFY, SO IT WOULD SUIT KASUMI PERFECTLY.
PLUS IT'S CHEAP!

GASP
THIS ONE WOULD SUIT SAKU!
PINK

CHEER
THEY HAVE MY FAVORITE COLOR, TOO!
SALE
SALE

I'LL BUY THEM ALL!
THESE, PLEASE!

WHOOSH
THE DOORS ARE CLOSING.

PHEW
ふ…
そわそわ
I NEED TO STAY AWAKE THIS TIME!
CLACK
ガタン
CLACK
ガタン
CLACK
ガ
AH...
ゴソゴソ
RUSTLE
いそいそ
FIDGET
FIDGET
TEE-HEE!
I'M SO SLEEPY...
WHY...
IS THERE ONLY ONE BED IN THEIR ROOM?
SAKU ONLY LET ME SLEEP WITH HER WHEN SHE WAS IN ELEMENTARY SCHOOL.
SHE'S TALENTED AT EVERYTHING AND IS RESPECTED BY EVERYONE...
BUT MY WONDERFUL OLDER SISTER HARDLY PAYS ATTENTION TO ME...

IT MAKES ME WANT TO TEASE HER.
TUG
つん
HEY!

ALTHOUGH OUR OLDEST SISTER, RIKO, IS AN EVEN BIGGER BULLY THAN ME...
けら
LAUGH
けら
LAUGH
I HATE YOU, RIKO!
SAKURAKO
RIKO
HINA

IS THAT WHY SHE CHOSE TO GO TO A HIGH SCHOOL FAR FROM HOME?
NO, PROBABLY NOT...

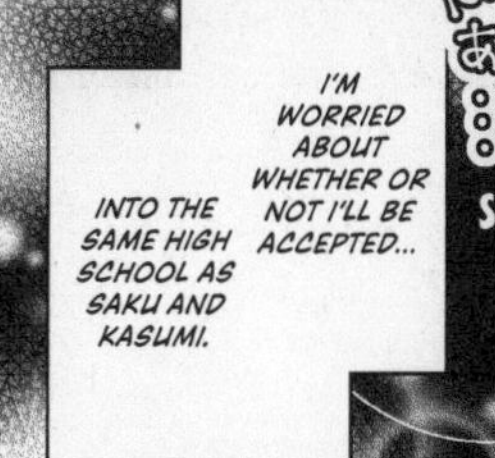
はぁ…
SIGH
I'M WORRIED ABOUT WHETHER OR NOT I'LL BE ACCEPTED...
INTO THE SAME HIGH SCHOOL AS SAKU AND KASUMI.

THAT SCHOOL IS TRADITIONALLY VERY LENIENT, BUT IT'S A HIGH-LEVEL SCHOOL AND MANY APPLICANTS MEANS A LOT OF COMPETITION.
I HONESTLY THINK IT'LL BE DIFFICULT WITH YOUR GRADES AS THEY ARE.

ピ
BEEP

WELL...
SINCE SAKU STARTED TUTORING ME...
MY GRADES IN JAPANESE AND ENGLISH HAVE GONE UP.

I'M SURE I'LL BE FINE.

POUR

UGH...
IT'S RAINING...

OH NO!
I DIDN'T BRING AN UMBRELLA WITH ME...
WHAT SHOULD I DO?

IT'S NOT RAINING THAT HARD, SO...
WAH...
SPLASH
パシャ
I'M FINE.
SPLASH
パシャ
I'M FINE.
SLIDE
SPLAT
AH!

AW...
HUH?
HINA?
コッ
CLACK
IT REALLY IS YOU, ISN'T IT?

KASUMI...
WINTER RAIN IS SO CHILLY...

ス
RUSTLE
YOU'RE SOAKED.
YOU MIGHT CATCH A COLD.

ザアアアアアアア
POUR
SAKURAKO TEXTED ME TO SAY THAT YOU STILL HAVEN'T ARRIVED.
AH...
YEAH, I'M A LITTLE LATE.
HA HA

UM...
WHAT ABOUT YOU?
I JUST GOT OFF WORK.
I WAS ON THE EARLY SHIFT.
ガチャッ
KER-CHAK
I'M HOME!
KASUMI! OH, AND HINAKO'S WITH YOU!
S-SORRY I'M LATE...
OH...
DIDN'T YOU HAVE AN UMBRELLA? YOU'RE SOAKED! GO TAKE A SHOWER.
HUH? BUT...
IT'S ONLY NOON...
JUST GO!
NOW!
SHOVE
OKAY...

ほか
STEAMY
ほか
STEAMY
LET'S EAT!
IS THIS LUNCH?
IT'S A CHICKEN-AND-EGG RICE BOWL...
FOR ME?
WERE YOU WAITING TO EAT UNTIL I GOT HERE?
WELL, YOU NEVER MESSAGED ME...
AND I MADE ENOUGH FOR THREE.
HURRY UP AND EAT!
AH...
THAT'S RIGHT. HERE...
RUSTLE

I SAW THESE AND THOUGHT THAT THEY MIGHT...
SUIT YOU TWO...
SO I BOUGHT THEM.
HERE YOU GO.
I HOPE YOU LIKE THEM!
チラ
GLANCE
KASUMI, LET'S GET MATCHING ONES! I WANT TO MATCH!
HUH?
ふふっ
CHUCKLE
THANKS.
I KNEW IT...
THEY'RE SO SIMILAR.

Chapter 27

THERE WAS A PETAL ON YOU.

OH...

ふーっ
PHEW
I FINISHED MAKING LUNCH!
WHERE SHOULD WE GO?
WOW! THERE ARE 5 TIERS!
パチ パチ
CLAP CLAP

DO YOU THINK WE CAN DO IT ON SCHOOL GROUNDS?
どーんっ
TA-DA!
LET'S ASK.
THERE'S A GIANT CHERRY BLOSSOM TREE BY THE SCHOOL GATE.

THAT'S FINE, AS LONG AS YOU CLEAN UP AFTER YOUR-SELVES.
WOW, YOU MADE ALL THAT?
WE WILL!

AH!
KASUMI!
WHAT ARE YOU DOING HERE?

WE'VE GOT PLENTY TO EAT!
YOU TWO SHOULD JOIN US!
YAY!
IF YOU'RE SURE...
コクコク
NOD NOD

OH, OH! LET US JOIN, TOO!
WE HAVE SNACKS AND JUICE!
ゾロ
CROWD

WE HEARD YOU'RE HAVING A PICNIC, SO WE ALSO BROUGHT SOME FOOD.
ゾロ
CROWD
HEY.

わいわい
CHATTER CHATTER
THERE ARE SO MANY PEOPLE NOW.
EVEN OUR TEACHER CAME...

HEY, TEACH. PLEASE LET US HAVE A SIP!
BOO
BOO
AS IF I WOULD. YOU KNOW IT'S NOT ALLOWED.
WAIT UNTIL YOU'RE OF AGE, KIDS.
BEER
BEER
JUICE

YOU'LL GET EXPELLED IF YOU DRINK.
YOU TOO, MIZUKI.
AW...
I'M NOT INTERESTED IN ALCOHOL.
WHO WANTS CHOCOLATE?
ME!
BEER

CHOMP
WHO WOULD BE STUPID ENOUGH TO DRINK IN A PLACE LIKE THIS?

TEE-HEE-HEE~!
KASUMIIIII!
WHOA...
SAKURAKO, YOUR FACE IS REALLY RED.
HUH?
SLUMP

HUH?
DID SHE GET DRUNK OFF THESE BOURBON CHOCOLATES?
?!
YOU'VE GOT TO BE KIDDING ME.
TOTALLY FINE
BWA-HA-HA!

I'VE NEVER SEEN SOMEONE GET DRUNK ON SUCH LITTLE ALCOHOL...
HA HA HA!
YOU OKAY, SAKURAKO?
SWAY
SWAY

SMOOCH

TUG
TUG
I CAN'T GET HER OFF...
?!
EEK
WOW...

ぷはっ
PHEW
CUT IT OUT!
TEE-HEE-HEE~!
WHAT ARE THEY DOING?
あわわ
FLUSTER

SERI, WANNA SMOOCH?
WH-WH-WH-WHAT?!

ポ
WHAM
OUCHIE!
カッ

はっ
GASP
WHOOPS! I JUST GOT SO IRRI-TATED...
I HIT YOU WITHOUT THINKING.
OUCHIE, OUCHIE!
HE-HE-HE, KASUMI!

JUST SLEEP UNTIL YOU SOBER UP.
BE A GOOD GIRL, OKAY?

STRETCH
へにゃ~
HE-HE~!

ぐりぐり
RUB
RUB
HEY...

KASUMI, YOUR THIGHS SMELL GOOD~!
STOP IT.
SMACK

*A SWEET, LOW- OR NON-ALCOHOLIC DRINK MADE OF FERMENTED RICE

I'VE ONLY EVER HAD AMAZAKE* DURING NEW YEAR'S, SO I HAD NO IDEA.
BETTER BE CAREFUL.
BUT YOU'RE FINE WITH AMAZAKE?

GASP
BUT DOES THAT MEAN...

THAT IF I GET DRUNK, I CAN KISS YOU AS MUCH AS I WANT?
ARE YOU SURE YOU'RE SOBER?
YOU'D BETTER NOT! NOT WHILE WE'RE UNDERAGE...

BY THE WAY, WE NEVER ACTUALLY PAID ATTENTION TO THE CHERRY BLOSSOMS, DID WE?

NOW THAT YOU MENTION IT...!

WHAT'S THE POINT OF EVEN GOING THEN?

TRASH

SOON WE'LL HAVE BEEN STAYING IN THE BOARDING HOUSE FOR A FULL YEAR.

I'M HOME!

WELCOME HOME!

I'VE GOTTEN USED TO COOKING AND CLEANING BY MYSELF.
チーン!!
DING

HOW-EVER...
すい LEAN
SERI!
OH, IT'S GRATIN.
!
いっ
ドキッ
BA-DUMP

AT FIRST I BOUGHT ALL OUR SIDE DISHES...
BUT I'VE LEARNED HOW TO COOK SOME MYSELF!

ドキドキ
BA-DUMP
CAN YOU BUY TOILET PAPER NEXT TIME YOU'RE AT THE STORE?
WE'RE ALMOST OUT!
I'M STILL NOT USED TO THE LACK OF SPACE WITH SHOUKO!
U-UNDER-STOOD.
LEASE GIVE ME SOME SPACE.

YOU ALWAYS TURN RED SO EASILY.
IT'S BECAUSE YOU'RE ALWAYS SO CLOSE!

BY THE WAY, WHEN ARE YOU GOING TO START TALKING TO ME LIKE WE'RE ACTUALLY FRIENDS?
YOU ALWAYS SOUND SO FORMAL.

DOES IT BOTHER YOU?
YEAH.
IT ALWAYS HAS.

MAYBE I'LL TRY IGNORING YOU UNTIL YOU DROP THE FORMALITIES!
HUH?
REALLY?

UM, UH...
LA-LA-LA~! ♪
FIDGET
オロオロ

H-HI...
SHOUKO?
GULP

TEARY
うーーー…
プルプル
TREMBLE
TREMBLE

ALL YOU HAVE TO DO IS LIGHTEN UP!
THAT'S EASY FOR YOU TO SAY!

I'VE NEVER ACTED THAT FAMILIAR WITH ANYONE BEFORE.

OH? WHAT ABOUT YOUR PARENTS?
I USED POLITE SPEECH.

AH! BUT THERE WAS ONE EXCEPTION...

MY FAMILY'S DOG!
HER NAME WAS SARAH!
THEN JUST PRETEND I'M YOUR DOG!
WOOF!

TO START WITH, YOU'VE ALWAYS BEEN SO CASUAL WITH ME!
HMM?
SHAA

TO ME, THAT WAS VERY DISCON-CERTING!

OKAY...
THEN I'LL CALL YOU MISS SERI! ♪

YOU'RE CUTE WHEN YOU'RE ANGRY, TOO.
PLEASE CUT IT OUT!
FOR HEAVEN'S SAKE!

IT'S BECAUSE I'M LIKE THIS THAT WE CAN'T BECOME CLOSE FRIENDS...
SNUGGLE
もぞ…

ひょこっ
PEEK

PRACTICE SPEAKING CASUALLY WITH ME!

...
HAVE A PLEASANT EVENING, SHOUKO.

CLASSES MAKE ME SO SLEEPY...
I WANTED TO NAP THROUGH ALL OF THEM.
HEY, NOW.
YOU DID SLEEP A LOT!

SHOUKO!
YOU FORGOT YOUR LUNCH!

THANKS!

DO THEY SEEM CLOSER THAN USUAL?
DID THEY ALWAYS CALL EACH OTHER BY THEIR FIRST NAMES?
THAT LUNCH BOX LOOKS HUGE...

BY THE WAY, WHY DO YOU ALWAYS ACT SO CASUAL WITH ME?
YOU DON'T EVEN ACT SO CLOSE WITH AZUSA AND THE OTHERS...
HMM...

I GUESS I DON'T REALLY HAVE A REASON.
OH, REALLY?

I JUST CAN'T IMAGINE TREATING YOU ANY OTHER WAY! ♡

YEAH, I GUESS IT WOULD BE WEIRD...
DOES THE ♡ HAVE A MEANING?
I FEEL LIKE EVERYONE IS MORE FORMAL WITH ME, THOUGH.

HI, KASUMI! ♡
HI, SAKURAKO! ♡
THAT'S KIND OF ANNOY-ING...
IT MAKES ME WANT TO IGNORE HER.

Illustration gallery of Yukiko

THE "IT HAS NO RELATION TO THE STORY ITSELF, BUT I'VE ALWAYS WANTED TO DRAW THEM LIKE THIS" SERIES #3
FRILL FESTIVAL

Futaribeya
A ROOM FOR TWO

Special Chapter #2 -
"The School's Seven Mysteries"
THAT CHINESE FOOD WAS GREAT.
YEAH!
KER-CHA
HUH?
IT'S SERI AND SHOUKO. WHAT ARE YOU GUYS DOING?
OH!
GOOD EVENING.
I FORGOT SOME-THING AT SCHOOL...
SO I WAS GONNA GO GET IT, BUT SERI STOPPED ME.
IT'S ALREADY 10 PM! WHY CAN'T YOU WAIT UNTIL MONDAY?
SERI FURUYASHIKI
SAKURAKO AND KASUMI'S NEXT-DOOR NEIGHBOR/ UNDERCLASSMAN
TODAY IS FRIDAY.
WELL...
I FORGOT MY HOMEWORK IN THE TRACK TEAM ROOM, BUT IT'S DUE MONDAY MORNING.
OHHH, GOTCHA.
SHOUKO AKASHI
SAME AS SERI
RATTLE

I HAVE A KEY TO THE SCHOOL, IF YOU NEED IT.
WHY DON'T YOU ALL GO TOGETHER?
NATSUKI HIYUUGA
THE BOARDING HOUSE'S LANDLORD
WAH!
YOU STILL HAVEN'T GONE HOME YET?
USUALLY YOU'RE NEVER HERE IN THE EVENINGS!
I JUST HAPPENED TO STAY BEHIND TODAY.
THE SCHOOL AT NIGHT, HUH?
CLINK
HERE YOU GO.
BE CAREFUL NOT TO RUN INTO...
THE SCHOOL'S SEVEN MYSTERIES!
...?
LET'S GO!

DOES OUR SCHOOL EVEN HAVE SEVEN MYSTERIES?
YEP! ONE OF THE TRACK MEMBERS TOLD ME ABOUT THEM.

SINCE WE'RE GOING...
WHY DON'T WE CHECK THEM OUT?
EXCITED
EXCITED

WHAAAT?
LET'S NOT!
IT'S TOO SCARY!
SHOUKO, YOU'RE NOT SCARED OF THAT KIND OF STUFF?
NOT AT ALL!
IS AFRAID

KASUMI!
ぎゅう
SQUEEZE
YOU CAN GO HOME IF YOU'RE SCARED.
IT'D BE SCARIER TO GO HOME BY MYSELF!
スタスタ
TAP
TAP
GEEZ!

ガチャ
KER-CHAK
IT'S SO DARK!
I CAN'T SEE...
I WONDER IF THE LIGHTS WILL WORK...
FLICK
OH...
THEY TURNED ON!
DO YOU THINK WE'LL GET IN TROUBLE?
SOMEONE WILL SEE...
DON'T YOU THINK SNEAKING AROUND IN THE DARK WOULD LOOK EVEN WORSE?
WELL... THAT'S TRUE...
OKAY!
LET'S START FROM THE CLOSEST PLACE!
LET'S GO CONQUER THE SEVEN MYSTERIES!
YAAAY.
HOW DID THINGS TURN OUT LIKE THIS?
SQUEAK
WHAT ABOUT YOUR HOMEWORK?
SQUEAK
THE GYM IS THE FURTHEST AWAY, SO WE CAN GO THERE LAST.
THE TRACK TEAM'S ROOM IS NEXT TO THE GYM.

THE FIRST RUMOR IS THAT THE BUSTS IN THE ART ROOM MOVE.
PLASTER BUSTS COST ANYWHERE FROM $500 TO $1000.
ズズ…
DRAG
WHAT?!
THEY'RE THAT EX-PENSIVE?
THIS IS MY FIRST TIME IN THE ART ROOM.
SHOUKO CHOSE A MUSIC CLASS
AND I NEVER REALLY HAD A REASON TO COME THIS WAY.
YOU SHOULD HAVE CHOSEN MUSIC, TOO.
I'M REALLY BAD AT IT.
WHAT'S WRONG, SAKURAKO?
IS SOMETHING BOTHERING YOU?
STARE
じー
HUH? OH, IT'S NOTHING.

WHAT?

I WAS JUST THINKING...
HOW MUCH IT MIGHT COST TO ORDER A PLASTER BUST...

ブツ
MUMBLE
FIRST I'D HAVE TO FIND SOMEONE TO MAKE THE MODEL...
WAIT, ACTUALLY...
IT MIGHT BE FASTER TO JUST STUDY IT MYSELF.
MARBLE MIGHT BE BEST TO RECREATE HER SKIN...
ブツ
MUMBLE
...WHAT ARE YOU TALKING ABOUT?

UM...
I WAS JUST THINKING IT'S WONDERFUL TO BE ABLE TO CAPTURE BEAUTY FOR ETERNITY. ♡
ぽっ
BLUSH
AN ETERNITY OF KASUMI...
OKAY...
I STILL DON'T GET IT.
DON'T LOOK TOO MUCH INTO IT...
L-LET'S MOVE ON!

THE SECOND RUMOR IS ABOUT THE "DOOR THAT CANNOT BE OPENED."

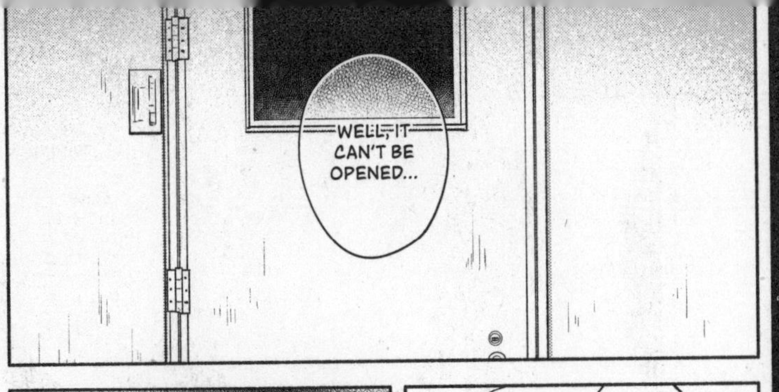

WELL, IT CAN'T BE OPENED...

BECAUSE IT DOESN'T HAVE A DOOR-KNOB!
A-HA-HA!
OF COURSE IT CAN'T OPEN!
SOMEONE PROBABLY STOLE IT...

IT'D BE SO SCARY TO BE LOCKED IN THERE...
SHIVER

IF THAT HAPPENED...
I'D KICK THE DOOR DOWN AND SAVE YOU.
BA-DUMP
KASUMI! WHAT WOULD YOU DO IF I WAS LOCKED INSIDE?
M-
MAYBE CALL A TEACHER?
SHE'S TOO REALISTIC!

THE THIRD RUMOR IS ABOUT A STAIRCASE THAT EXPANDS TO HAVE 13 STEPS.
WHICH OF THE STAIRCASES IS IT?
IT SHOULD BE THIS ONE.
OKAY!
THEN LET'S GO!
ONE...
TWO, THREE...
TAP
FOUR...
TAP
FIVE, SIX...
SEVEN, EIGHT...
TAP
NINE...
TEN!
THUNK
...ONLY TEN STEPS, HUH?
YEAH...
BUT THERE ARE NO STEPS BETWEEN ME AND KASUMI!
WHAT ARE YOU ALKING BOUT?

THE FOURTH RUMOR IS REGARDING YOUR REFLECTION IN THE MIRROR IN THE DANCE STUDIO.
IF YOU LOOK AT YOURSELF IN THIS MIRROR AT 2 AM, THE FOURTH REFLECTION WILL SHOW YOUR FUTURE SELF...
OR SO THEY SAY.
THERE JUST HAPPENS TO BE ANOTHER MIRROR HERE, SO GO RIGHT AHEAD, SAKURAKO!
HUH?!
I HAVE TO DO IT?!
WHY?
I'LL HOLD IT FOR YOU.
UGH... WELL, IF IT'S JUST LOOKING IN THE MIRROR...
PLUS IT'S NOT 2 AM YET...
WELL?
THERE ARE LOTS OF KASUMIS IN THE MIRRORS!
IS THIS HEAVEN?
HUH?

THE FIFTH RUMOR SAYS THE PIANO IN THE MUSIC ROOM CAN PLAY ITSELF...
MUSIC ROOM
I... CAN HEAR THE PIANO...
I CAN'T BELIEVE IT...
WAAAH!
ガラ
RATTLE
N-
MISS NATSUKI?!
?!
パ
BRIGHT
I THOUGHT I'D SNEAK AROUND AND COME IN HERE TO SURPRISE YOU! ☆
PLEASE DON'T!

THE SIXTH RUMOR SAYS THAT YOU CAN HEAR THE SOUND OF A BALL BOUNCING IN THE GYM.
WE'RE FINALLY AT THE GYM!
*NATSUKI WENT HOME.
I'LL JUST GO AND GRAB MY HOMEWORK.
I'M TIRED...
DASH
THERE AREN'T ANY BALLS AROUND.
GLANCE
I DON'T HEAR ANYTHING, EITHER.
GLANCE
GOOD! IT CAN STAY THAT WAY!
SORRY TO KEEP YOU WAITING!
THAT WAS FAST!
I FOUND A PING PONG BALL ON MY WAY THERE.
THAT'S NOT THE BALL FROM THE RUMOR, IS IT?
IF IT BOUNCES...
TOSS
CLONK
TAP
TAP
I'M SURE IT'S DIFFERENT...

はぁ～
I'M TIRED... LET'S LEAVE.
SIGH
HUH?
1, 2, 3, 4... WE ONLY WENT AROUND TO 6 OF THE 7 MYSTERIES!
I FORGOT ONE.
REALLY?
WHAT'S THE LAST ONE?
UM...
OH, IT'S THAT! THE STATUE OF KINJIROU NINOMIYA CAN RUN.
うおぉぉ おぉぉ
WHOOO
じーーーっ
SILENCE
...
DID OUR SCHOOL EVEN HAVE A STATUE OF HIM TO BEGIN WITH?
I'VE NEVER SEEN IT BEFORE.
NO, IT'S DOESN'T!
HA-HA-HA
あはは
ISN'T THE STATUE WE HAVE REALLY WEIRD?
HUH?
WHO MADE A STATUE LIKE THIS?
CACKLE CACKLE
ケラケラ
STATUE OF VICTORY

I'M TURNING THE LIGHTS OFF.
OKAY!
FLICK
THE SCHOOL AT NIGHT REALLY IS CREEPY...
ARE YOU SCARED?
YEAH.
SO I'M GONNA STICK TO YOU!
WHOA!
FWAP
ガ
ば
THEY SURE ARE CLOSE.
GIGGLE
クス
GIGGLE
クス
HEY, YOU'RE HEAVY.
SERI, YOU DON'T SEEM TO BE SCARED.

I'M NOT THAT AFRAID OF THE DARK.
BUT GHOSTS FRIGHTEN ME.
HMM...
IN THAT CASE...

SQUEEZE

HEY!
I SAID I'M NOT SCARED!
ARE YOU CERTAIN YOU'RE NOT FAKING IT?!
I'M THE ONE WHO'S SCARED!
LET'S GO HOME!

MONDAY MORNING...
AH!
MISS NATSUKI!
OFFICE

THANKS FOR YOUR HELP ON FRIDAY!

HMM? WHAT HELP?
MORNING!
WE WENT AND VISITED ALL SEVEN OF THE MYSTERIES!
THEY WEREN'T THAT SCARY, WERE THEY?
AT LEAST THERE WEREN'T ANY SUPERNATURAL PHENOMENON.
YOU WERE THE SCARIEST PART.
IT WAS SCARY!

HUH? WHAT ARE YOU GUYS TALKING ABOUT?

I MEAN HOW...

YOU LENT US THE KEYS TO THE SCHOOL ON FRIDAY NIGHT...

THE KEYS TO THE SCHOOL? I DON'T HAVE THOSE.
ALSO, I HAD PLANS FRIDAY NIGHT, SO I LEFT AT 7 PM.
HUH?
WHAAAT?!
NOW THAT YOU MENTION IT, USUALLY EACH CLASSROOM IS LOCKED AS WELL...
I DIDN'T THINK ANYTHING OF IT.
THAT'S SO STRANGE...
N-N-NOOOO!

Chapter 28

BLUSH てれっ
CONGRATULATIONS ON BEING ACCEPTED...
TO OUR SCHOOL...
HINAKO!
CLAP パチ
CLAP パチ
CLAP パチ
CLAP パチ

I'M GLAD YOU DIDN'T HAVE ANY PROBLEMS GETTING IN.
YEAH, ME TOO.
IT WAS A CLOSE CALL...

OH, YEAH.
WHAT KIND OF PRESENT DO YOU WANT TO CELEBRATE?
HUH?

TH-THEN...
I WANT YOU, KASUMI!

HUH?
HUH?
EEK キャー
HEY...

IT'S YOUR FIRST DAY HERE, AND YOU'RE ALREADY TALKING LIKE THAT?
AH...
FUJIHO!
WHO'S THAT?

OH, UM...
THIS IS MY OLDER SISTER AND HER ROOMMATE, KASUMI.
FIDGET
FUJIHO IS MY ROOMMATE.
FIDGET
I'M FUJIHO KANOU.
NICE TO MEET YOU.
GOOD LUCK ROOMING WITH HER...
FIDGET

MY NAME IS SAKURAKO. PLEASE TAKE CARE OF HINAKO!

LOOKS LIKE YOUR OLDER SISTER GOT ALL THE INTELLIGENCE.
HEY!
WHAT DO YOU MEAN BY THAT?
ぷんっ HMPH
POOR THING...

WE HAVEN'T FINISHED CLEANING UP THE ROOM, SO LET'S GO BACK.
WHAAAT?
KASUMI, I'LL SEE YOU AGAIN SOON!

HINAKO IS REALLY SHY, BUT SHE SEEMS CLOSE WITH HER ROOMMATE ALREADY...
THAT'S STRANGE...
ISN'T IT A GOOD THING?

AH...
SHE NEVER TOLD ME WHAT KIND OF PRESENT SHE WANTED.
YOU DON'T NEED TO GIVE HER ONE!
ばっ

HINA LIVES ON THE 6TH FLOOR... I WOULD HATE LIVING THERE.
ALL THOSE STAIRS...
WAIT, WHAT?
THAT'S THE ONLY REASON?!

THE NEXT DAY...
THE ENTRANCE CEREMONY IS TODAY! LET'S CHECK OUT ALL THE NEW STUDENTS!
OKAY!

OH? THERE ARE SOME FLASHY GIRLS.
WHERE?

THOSE TWO!

THEY'RE SO ALIKE...
HINA...
WOW...

I CAN'T BELIEVE THIS IS OUR LAST YEAR. TIME SURE FLIES!
HIGH SCHOOL WILL BE OVER IN A FLASH.

WE HAVEN'T REALLY DONE A LOT OF "STUDENT-Y" THINGS, HAVE WE?
YOU'RE RIGHT.

SINCE WE ONLY HAVE A YEAR LEFT, LET'S DO OUR BEST TO ACT LIKE PROPER HIGH SCHOOL GIRLS!

NO...
WE NEED TO STUDY TO GET INTO COLLEGE.
NO! DON'T MAKE ME FACE REALITY!

KASUMI, DO YOU KNOW WHAT YOU'RE GOING TO DO AFTER YOU GRADUATE?
I HAVE A BASIC IDEA, YEAH.

HOPEFULLY I'LL BE ABLE TO GET INTO A NATIONAL PUBLIC SCHOOL WITH A RECOMMENDATION...

GIRK
YOU REALLY THINK YOU'LL GET ONE?
WILL YOU BE OKAY?
LOOK.
THESE ARE MY GRADES FOR THIS SEMESTER.
FLAP

HUH?
THEY'RE PRETTY HIGH!
WHEN DID YOU GET SO SMART?
WELL?
IT'S BECAUSE SHE'S GOT ME!

EATING LUNCH IN THE CAFETERIA
WHAT ABOUT YOU, SAKURAKO?
STILL HAVEN'T DECIDED?
YEAH...

MY TEACHER TOLD ME TO START BY APPLYING TO PLACES WITH A HIGH STANDARD SCORE...
BUT TO BE HONEST...

I CAN'T FIND ANYTHING I WANT TO DO MORE THAN JUST BEING WITH YOU!

THEN WHY NOT GO TO THE SAME UNIVERSITY?
AS ME, I MEAN.
WAIT, REALLY?
I THOUGHT YOU WOULDN'T LIKE THAT!

WELL...
WE HAVE TIME TO THINK UNTIL OUR PARENT-TEACHER CONFERENCES IN MAY.
YEAH!

AH.
CAMPUS LIFE!
KASUMI!

HAVE YOU HAD DINNER YET? WANT TO COME EAT WITH US?
ARE YOU SURE? YAY!
HA-HA-HA-!
YAY!
YAY!
AWESOME.

I'VE GOT SO MUCH ENERGY RIGHT NOW!
BRING IT ON, ENTRANCE EXAMS!
OH, UH, REALLY?

WELCOME TO THE BOARDING HOUSE!

I FEEL SO LAZY IN SPRING...
ROLL
ゴロ
ROLL
ゴロ
YOU SAY THAT EVERY MONTH.

IT'S FINE. ANYONE CAN DO IT!
I'LL JUST LET THEM KNOW.
BUT...

I WONDER IF I'LL BE OKAY...
I'M WORRIED.
I'LL SEND A MESSAGE TO SAY I'VE ARRIVED.

10 MINUTES LATER...
PANT
WHEEZE
YOU'RE MISS KAWAWA?! SORRY TO KEEP YOU WAITING!
PANT
WHEEZE

KASUMI ALWAYS SHOWS UP AT THE LAST MINUTE, SO I GOT CARELESS...
IT'S FINE...
KASUMI...

IT'S ACTUALLY PRETTY HARD TO SIT QUIETLY FOR THIS LONG.
HAD TO PUT HER HAIR UP
SCRITCH
SCRITCH
SCRITCH

DURING BREAK...
DID YOU GET SLEEPY? YOU MUST BE BORED!
HERE'S SOME COFFEE.
THANK YOU VERY MUCH!

I WAS A LITTLE SLEEPY AT FIRST...

BUT I WAS FINE AFTER I STARTED DAY-DREAMING!
HUH?
...?
DAYDREAMING...?

HERE'S YOUR PAYCHECK!
THANKS FOR TODAY! YOU REALLY HELPED US OUT!
OH, IT WAS NO PROBLEM.

I HAVE TIME UNTIL I'M SUPPOSED TO MEET KASUMI...
WHAT SHOULD I DO?
*KASUMI'S WORKING AT THE CAKE SHOP.

I GUESS I'LL GO TO THE LIBRARY.
I THINK THERE'S ONE NEAR HERE.

HUH? YUKARI?
AH!
SAKURAKO?

GEEZ!
KASUMI, YOU DRANK TOO MUCH!
YAWN
ふあぁ…

DROWSY
トローン
WELL, AN UPPER-CLASSMAN FROM MY SEMINAR INVITED ME OUT, SO I COULDN'T REFUSE...
ヒック
HICCUP

WOBBLE
ヨロ
ヨロ
WOBBLE
GET A HOLD OF YOURSELF! WE'RE GOING HOME NOW, SO HOLD ONTO ME.

AS IF! HA HA HA...
SOMEONE SAY SOMETHING TO HER...
SMILE
ニヤ
SMILE
ニヤ
IS SHE OKAY...?

CAN I SIT HERE?
THIS IS OUR FIRST TIME MEETING OUTSIDE OF SCHOOL!
Y-YEAH!

DO YOU COME HERE OFTEN?
SOMETIMES. IT'S A BIG LIBRARY.

OUR SCHOOL'S LIBRARY IS SO SMALL.

I'VE READ ALL THE BOOKS THERE ALREADY...
WAIT, REALLY? ALL OF THEM?!
PLEASE BE QUIET

OH, YOU'RE REVIEWING OLD TEST QUESTIONS? YOU WANT TO GO TO X UNIVERSITY?
PAST TEST QUESTIONS X UNIVERSITY

Y-YES, IT'S THE ONLY SCHOOL I'VE FOUND SO FAR...
ALTHOUGH IT MAY BE HARD TO GET IN TO...
KASUMI AND I WANT TO GO THERE, TOO!
PLEASE BE QUIET

HUH?
REALLY?
YEP! LET'S WORK HARD TOGETHER!
THEY'RE GOING TO GO TO THE SAME COLLEGE?
THAT'S AMAZING...

SO WE'RE AIMING TO GET INTO THE SAME SCHOOL... THAT MAKES ME A LITTLE NERVOUS...
I WONDER WHY...

SAKURAKO, SORRY TO KEEP YOU WAITING.
KASUMI!

OH, YUKARI.
ARE YOU LEAVING SOON? WANT TO GO HOME TOGETHER?
NOD
NOD
NOD

WERE YOU STUDYING?
I CAN'T FOCUS IN THE DORMS...
THAT LIBRARY IS NICE AND CLEAN, TOO!

SEE YOU LATER!

ALL RIGHT! I'LL DO MY BEST!

CLENCH

Illustration gallery of Yukiko

Futaribeya
A ROOM FOR TWO

Chapter 29

PARENT-TEACHER CONFERENCES TAKE PLACE TODAY.

THANK YOU VERY MUCH.

WITH SAKURAKO'S GRADES, I DON'T THINK SHE'LL HAVE A PROBLEM...
NO MATTER WHAT UNIVERSITY SHE APPLIES TO.

YOU KNOW WHERE YOU WANT TO APPLY TO, RIGHT?
YES.
WHAT WILL YOU MAJOR IN?
I'M STILL NOT SURE...

HOW DID YOU DECIDE WHAT TO STUDY?
I... JUST PICKED AT RANDOM.
DON'T USE ME AS A ROLE MODEL.

WHAT ABOUT YOU, MOM?
I PUT A COUPLE DIFFERENT OPTIONS IN A HAT AND JUST PULLED ONE AT RANDOM!
THAT REALLY BRINGS ME BACK!
IN ANY CASE, THINK OF SOMETHING BY OUR NEXT MEETING.

SIGH はぁ~
WHAT SHOULD I DO?
HEY, I WANT TO MEET KASUMI!

UM...
I THINK SHE'S EATING LUNCH RIGHT NOW.
IN OUR CLASSROOM...
SAKURAKO, IS YOUR MEETING OVER?
ひょこっ PEEK

AH!
IT'S KASUMI!

SH-SHE'S SO TINY...
UM... YOU MUST BE SAKURAKO'S MOM.
IT'S SO NICE TO MEET YOU!
4 FT 9 IN

I'VE ALWAYS WANTED TO SAY HI BUT NEVER HAD A CHANCE.
I'M SORRY IT TOOK SO LONG FOR ME TO GREET YOU.

THANK YOU FOR TAKING CARE OF SAKU-RAKO.
BOW
OH NO, I'M THE ONE RE-CEIVING ALL THE CARE...
YOU DID A GREAT JOB RAISING HER.

PLEASE COME AND VISIT ANY TIME YOU'D LIKE!
I COULDN'T SEE YOU LAST TIME YOU CAME.
RIGHT?
YEP!

I WOULDN'T MIND HAVING YOU AS A DAUGHTER-IN-LAW!
YOU CAN MARRY KAKERU!
?!
GAPE
M-MOM, WHAT ARE YOU EVEN SAYING?!

GEEZ!
DON'T JOKE AROUND ABOUT STUFF LIKE THAT!

I JUST THOUGHT IT'D BE NICE TO HAVE A GIRL LIKE KASUMI IN THE FAMILY...
THERE'S NO NEED TO YELL.

YANK
HA HA HA!
I WOULDN'T MIND MAKING SAKURAKO MY WIFE.

THAT'S FINE TOO! WHATEVER WORKS FOR YOU!
OH!
KA-
KA-SUMI?!

AH...
I HAVE PLANS TO MEET FRIENDS FOR LUNCH...
SO I'LL SEE YOU TWO LATER!

YOUR MOM IS AMAZ-ING... ALL THAT ENERGY...
SHE'S A NATURAL AIRHEAD.
AT LEAST CHANGE OUT OF YOUR PAJAMAS FIRST...!

WHAT ABOUT YOUR MOM?
SHE'LL BE COMING AFTER CLASSES END.
I STILL HAVE TIME!

ISN'T THAT HER, THOUGH?
HUH?!
DING
DONG
DANG
DONG
MOM?!
PANT
PANT

WOBBLE
SOME-THING CAME UP AND I HAVE TO WORK TONIGHT. DO YOU THINK WE CAN HAVE OUR MEET-ING NOW?
WOBBLE
YOU SHOULD HAVE LET ME KNOW.
OUR LUNCH BREAK IS ALREADY OVER...

RATTLE
MY CLASS IS NEXT, SO IT'S FINE.
I'LL JUST ASSIGN SELF-STUDY.
FWAP
PLEASE DO!

KASUMI WANTS TO GO TO UNIVER-SITY...
THAT'S FINE.
ABOUT THE REC-OMMEN-DATION...
KASUMI, WORK HARD AND DO YOUR BEST.
SNAP
SNAP

FIVE MINUTES LATER...
SEE YOU LATER!
DASH
WHAT WAS THE POINT IN COMING?

AH...
THAT WAS FAST!
PAT
WELL, SHE DIDN'T REALLY DISAGREE ABOUT ANYTHING.

SIGH
I WONDER WHAT I SHOULD MAJOR IN...

WHAT ABOUT YOU, KASUMI?
HAVE YOU DECIDED?
IT'S A SECRET.

HUH? WHY?!
BECAUSE YOU'D PROBABLY WANT TO MAJOR IN IT, TOO.
URK

I NEED TO HURRY UP AND GET BACK TO WORK!

I CAN'T BELIEVE I WORE MY PAJAMA PANTS OUTSIDE...

CLACK

CLACK

WHAT ARE YOU MAKING?
PSSH
プシュ
HOMEMADE LEMONADE!

GULP
ゴクゴク
THIS WEEK I'M TAKING TIME OFF MY JOBS AND CRAM SCHOOL.

HM?
SLIDE
ずる
ずる
SLIDE

YOU'VE BEEN REALLY BUSY RECENTLY, AFTER ALL.
PHEW
ぷはー
I'M A LITTLE TIRED...

FWUMP
ゴテッ
GOOD NIGHT.
YOU'LL CATCH A COLD IF YOU DON'T PUT SOME CLOTHES ON.
HUH?

RING
AH... IT'S AZUSA.
RING

HELLO?
SAKURAKO, ARE YOU FREE? CAN YOU TUTOR ME?
I'LL BUY YOU DINNER!
SURE, I'M FR—

STARE
...
HER EYES ARE SAYING, "YOU'RE LEAVING ME?"
OR SO SAKURAKO THINKS.

SORRY, TODAY'S NOT GOOD FOR ME. MAYBE NEXT TIME!
OKAY!
WHAT IS THIS?
SHE'S SO CUTE...

DING
HMM?
DONG

KASUMI, IT'S HINA! I CAME OVER TO HANG OUT! ♡

DING
...
HINA...
DONG

DING
SAKU? ANYONE THERE?
I'LL JUST PRETEND NO ONE'S HOME.
YEP.
DONG

I GUESS THEY'RE NOT HOME...
NO ONE'S ANSWERING.

GOING TO HANG OUT WITH YOUR OLDER SISTER ON THE WEEK-ENDS...
DON'T YOU HAVE ANY FRIENDS?
OR DO YOU HAVE A SISTER COMPLEX?

I DON'T REALLY NEED FRIENDS.
PLUS I'M SHY.
I PROBABLY WOULDN'T GET ALONG WITH MY CLASS-MATES ANYWAY.

I'M HAPPIER JUST BEING ABLE TO GAZE AT KASUMI. ♡
SAKURAKO KAWAWA
KASUMI YAMABUKI
WOW...

THIS IS BAD... MY LEGS ARE GETTING PINS AND NEEDLES...
TINGLE

zzz...
BUT KASUMI IS SLEEP-ING...
I DON'T WANT TO WAKE HER UP.

TELEKINESIS WOULD BE CONVE-NIENT AT TIMES LIKE THESE...
HIYAH!
zzz...
FLOAT

SIT UP
I'M THIRSTY...
NEED A DRINK...
IT'S LIKE SHE READ MY MIND...

KASUMI, I SHOULD START MAKING DINNER SOON...
STRETCH
MMPH...

SLOWLY
WHY DON'T WE ORDER PIZZA TONIGHT? THAT'S MUCH EASIER.

RIGHT?

SHE PULLED OUT THE PUPPY EYES!
RING
HELLO! MAY I TAKE YOUR ORDER?
WHIP

ISN'T THIS MOVIE SCARY?
NO, I DON'T THINK SO.
BORROWED THE DVD FROM SUZU
CRASH

HERE.
HUH? OH...
AHHH...
I CAN EAT BY MYSELF...
OO PIZZA

AH.
SHOVE

HEY! IF YOU'RE GOING TO FEED ME, DO IT RIGHT!
HAHA...
YOU GOT MY SHIRT DIRTY!

SIGH
NOW I'M FULLY CHARGED.
ふぁぁ
BURP
MAYBE I'LL TAKE ANOTHER SHOWER!...

FULLY CHARGED?
FROM JUST LAYING AROUND?
?

I WAS CHARGING MYSELF WITH SAKURAKO ENERGY.

I SEE...
KASUMI'S FLIRTING IS BAD FOR MY HEART...
ははは
HA HA HA

THEY ATE TWO LARGE PIZZAS BY THEMSELVES...

ATE MOST OF THEM HERSELF.

YOU HAVE TO HAVE ICE CREAM AFTER EATING PIZZA!

ICE CREAM

カラ
EMPTY

○○PIZZA

○○PIZZA

Illustration gallery of Yukiko

SUIT COSPLAYS THAT
KIND OF LOOK LIKE
SECRET AGENTS.

Futaribeya
A ROOM FOR TWO

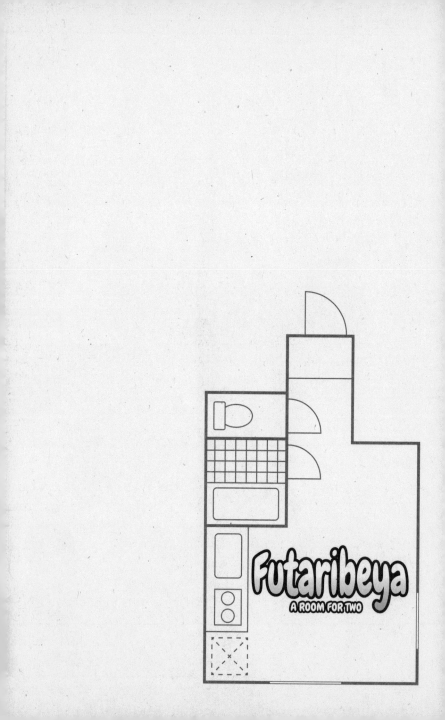

Chapter 30

I'M FULL...
CAN'T EAT ANYMORE.
CLACK
カチャ
?!

IT'S TOO MUCH WORK TO MOVE MY JAW.
SO HOT...
SLUMP
I'M SLEEPY...

IT'S TRUE THAT IT GOT HOT PRACTICALLY OVERNIGHT...
I KNOW YOU'RE USUALLY SLUGGISH TO BEGIN WITH, BUT ARE YOU SURE YOU'RE NOT SICK?

ISN'T IT JUST SENIOR-ITIS?
YOU KNOW, SINCE IT'S OUR LAST YEAR.
I'VE BEEN WORKING TOO HARD RECENTLY...
TRYING TO LIVE A SERIOUS LIFE.

DO YOU WANT TO HAVE NOODLES FOR DINNER?
WOULD THAT BE EASIER TO EAT?
SAKU-RAKO, YOU SHOULDN'T SPOIL HER.

SOMETIMES IT UPSETS ME WHEN I SEE YOU DOING THAT.
LIKE YOU'RE BABYING HER.

AND I THINK YOU SHOULD RETURN THE FAVOR MORE OFTEN, KASUMI.
PAT
HUH?
IT'S FINE! I GET STRESSED WHEN PEOPLE TRY TO THANK ME!

WHAT?
I'M HAPPY AS LONG AS KASUMI ACCEPTS ME INTO HER LIFE.

AH...
WHAT WERE YOU SAYING? I WASN'T LISTENING.
HUH?
SHOCK

HEY... YAMABUKI.
OH, IT'S THE TEACHER.

THERE'LL BE A CLASS ON HOW TO WRITE ESSAYS ASKING FOR RECOMMEN-DATIONS, SO YOU SHOULD TAKE IT.
FLAP
HERE'S THE APPLICATION FORM.

HUH...?

I DON'T THINK STUDENTS CAN WRITE THEIR OWN RECOMMEN-DATIONS...
THAT'S NOT WHAT I SAID.
LISTEN PROPERLY FOR ONCE.

I'VE LOST ALL MY ENERGY AND MOTI-VATION..
UGH...

I WONDER WHAT WOULD HELP YOU GET YOUR ENERGY BACK.
USUALLY YOU PERK UP JUST BY SEEING FOOD.

WHAT DO YOU TWO DO?
I USUALLY EXERCISE WHEN I'M IN A BAD MOOD.
I DEFINITELY DON'T WANT TO DO THAT.

AZUSA IS ALWAYS ENER-GETIC SO HER MOODS RUB OFF ON ME.
IT'S ALL THANKS TO ME!
YOU'RE SO LOUD, AZUSA...

SO HOT...
I KNOW!
I JUST THOUGHT OF A GREAT IDEA!
CLATTER

SAKU-RAKO, GO BUY SOME ICE CUBES AT THE SCHOOL STORE!
I'LL BE RIGHT BACK!
DASH

WHAT IS SHE GOING TO DO WITH ICE?
MAYBE COOL HER HEAD?
WHO KNOWS?
ICE CUBES
EXTRA!
BOUGHT IT ANYWAY
TAP
TAP
TA-DA! AN ELEC-TRIC ICE SHAVER!
RATTLE
I BROUGHT IT FROM MY ROOM!
WOW...

YOU JUST HAVE TO PUT THE ICE IN THE MACHINE...
CLACK
ICE
EXTRA

GRIND GRIND GRIND GRIND
ガリガリガリガリ
リガリガリガリガ
GRIND GRIND GRIND GRIND
WHAT'S SHE DOING?

ガリガリガリ
ISN'T IT A LITTLE LOUD?
WE'RE STILL ON LUNCH BREAK, SO IT'S FINE!

ガリガリガリ
GRIND GRIND GRIND
PLUS, KASUMI LOOKS HAPPY.
MAKE MINE A LARGE...
SHAVED ICE...

GRIND
TEACHER ▶
RATTLE
ガラッ
HEY!
YOU CAN'T BE THIS LOUD JUST BECAUSE IT'S BREAK TIME!
GRIND
GRIND
GRIND
AH...

WHAT ARE YOU DOING?
WE'RE EATING SHAVED ICE!
わい
CHEER
わい
CHEER
IT'S GREAT!
HEY, NOW. YOU SHOUL
KNOW...
THAT YOU CAN'T BRING THAT INTO THE CLASS-ROOM.
SORRY!

BY THE WAY, IS THERE ENOUGH FOR ME?
WHAT FLAVORS OF SYRUP ARE THERE?
AH... SO YOU JUST WANTED SOME.

I GOT BRAIN FREEZE...

I WANT TO EAT AN ENTIRE BUCKET OF SHAVED ICE!

キーン

THROB

SERI, WANT TO GO SOMEWHERE TOMORROW?

TOMORROW?
YOU MEAN SATURDAY?
SHE ALWAYS HAS CLUB ACTIVITIES ON THE WEEKENDS, THOUGH...

OR WOULD YOU RATHER NOT?

OH, YEAH...
OUR CLUB PRACTICE WAS SUDDENLY CANCELED...
SO I THOUGHT IT'D BE NICE IF WE COULD GO SOMEWHERE TOGETHER!

IT'S FINE. LET'S GO.
ALL RIGHT! JUST LET ME KNOW WHERE YOU WANT TO GO!
HUH?

GOING OUT WITH SHOUKO ON THE WEEK-END...
IT'S A FIRST FOR US.

WE'VE GONE SHOP-PING FOR GROCERIES BEFORE...
BUT I WONDER WHERE ELSE WE CAN GO...
AH.
SERI!
OH! HELLO, KASUMI.

WHERE I GO WITH SAKURAKO? I JUST LET HER CHOOSE.
?

OH, I SEE...
I PICKED THE WRONG PERSON TO ASK...

THE NEXT DAY...
DID YOU DECIDE WHERE YOU WANT TO GO?
コクコク
NOD
NOD

ARE YOU SURE WE CAN GO ANYWHERE I WANT?
YEP.

WE CAN GO WHEREVER YOU WISH, MY LADY.
ヒソ
WHISPER

GOODNESS!
WE'RE IN PUBLIC!
PLEASE DON'T DO THAT!
FWAP
パシッ
HAHA!
THE BUS IS HERE.

WOW!
IT'S THE OCEAN!
SPLASH

THE BEACH?
SO THIS IS WHERE YOU WANTED TO VISIT?
IS THAT WEIRD?

NOPE.
I WAS EXPECTING YOU TO SAY SHOPPING OR A MU-SEUM, SO I WAS JUST SURPRISED.
IT'S NOT WEIRD.
THE BREEZE FEELS GREAT!
WHOOSH

NOPE, IT'S NOT WEIRD AT ALL!
STRETCH
WHY DO YOU KEEP SAYING THAT...?

I'VE NEVER COME TO THE BEACH WITH CLASSMATES BEFORE.
SPLASH

I THOUGHT HIGH SCHOOL-ERS USUALLY COME TO THE BEACH...
I JUST NEVER HAD THE CHANCE...
NOW THAT YOU MENTION IT...

IT'S MY FIRST TIME COMING WITH A CLASS-MATE, TOO.
BUT I GUESS IT IS A TYPICAL SPOT FOR HIGH SCHOOLERS...
I ACTUALLY DON'T COME THAT OFTEN.
CLACK

IS THAT WHAT YOU DO HERE?
YEP!
TAKE THAT!
UWAH!
SPLASH

SERI, YOUR LEGS ARE SO PALE.
AND THEY LOOK SMOOTH.
SPLASH
SPLASH

IT'S BECAUSE I DON'T USUALLY WEAR SKIRTS OR SHORTS...
PLEASE DON'T STARE AT ME LIKE THAT...

IT MAKES YOU LOOK UNHEALTHY, SO YOU SHOULD TAN THEM TODAY!
NOOO!
FWAP

WH-WHY DO YOU ALWAYS DO STUFF LIKE THAT?!
YOU LOOKED LIKE YOU COULD USE A GOOD SKIRT FLIP.

I ACTUALLY DON'T LIKE THE FEELING OF SAND MOVING UNDER MY FEET...
SPLASH
SPLASH

OH...
IT TICKLES, DOESN'T IT?
I CAN'T SAY I ENJOY IT, EITHER.
FWAP
FWAP

I THOUGHT YOU'D BE USED TO IT.
HUH? WHY?

BECAUSE I IMAGINED YOUR HOUSE HAVING THOSE FLOORS THAT MOVE!
AND ESCALATORS AND STUFF!
LIKE THIS!
WHIR
THAT'S NOT SIMILAR TO SAND, AND WHO WOULD EVEN HAVE THOSE IN THEIR HOME?

AH... THAT FELT GREAT!
DO YOU FEEL BETTER NOW?

FEEL BETTER?
YES.
WHAT DO YOU MEAN?

YOUR CLUB DIDN'T ACTUALLY HAVE A BREAK THIS WEEKEND, DID IT?

... SO YOU KNEW?
TEE-HEE.

SUNDAY...

SHOUKO, YOU LOOK LIKE YOU'RE IN A GOOD MOOD! IS IT BECAUSE YOU SKIPPED PRACTICE YESTERDAY?

MY LIPS ARE SEALED!

Illustration gallery of Yukiko

Futaribeya
A ROOM FOR TWO

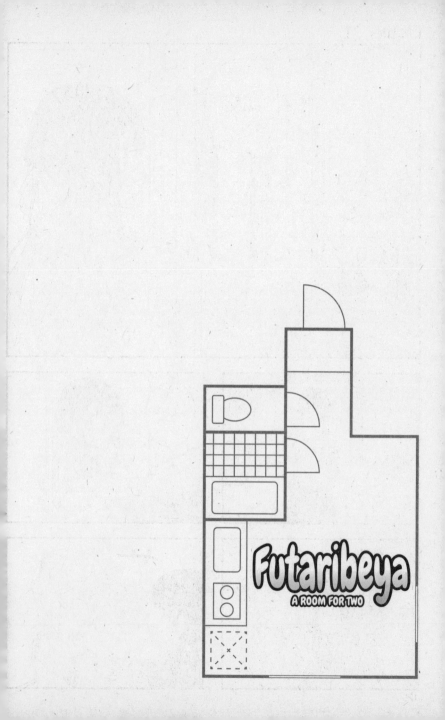

Chapter 31

AH...

IT'S SHOUKO.

I JUST REALIZED THAT SHOUKO HAS FRIENDS OTHER THAN ME...
IT MADE ME FEEL A LITTLE GLOOMY...

I WONDER IF THIS IS A TYPE OF JEALOUSY.
DO YOU EVER FEEL THIS WAY?

HM...
SOMETIMES I DO...
BUT AS LONG AS OTHER PEOPLE KNOW I'M SUPER CLOSE WITH THAT PERSON AND I'M THE ONE THEY SPEND ALL THEIR TIME WITH, I'M FINE.

WHY ARE YOU LOOKING AT ME?
SMILE
SMILE
...NO REASON.

I'VE NEVER THOUGHT OF IT THAT WAY BEFORE.

I DON'T REALLY CARE WHO GETS ALONG WITH WHOM.
THERE'S NO PARTICULAR RANK, EITHER...

BUT WOULDN'T YOU BE HAPPY KNOWING THAT THE PERSON YOU LIKE LIKES YOU BACK?
SLIDE
WHOA...

RIGHT?!
UH...
YEAH, I GUESS?
SH- SHE'S SO STRONG!

YOU HAVE OTHER CLASSMATES YOU'RE CLOSE WITH, RIGHT?
SINCE THE CLASSES DON'T CHANGE EACH YEAR.

DO YOU HANG OUT WITH SHOUKO IN THE CLASS-ROOM?
AH...
UM...
...

SHE ALWAYS SPENDS TIME WITH THE GIRLS ON THE TRACK TEAM...
OH...

I'M NOT GOOD AT MAKING FRIENDS.
I NEVER KNOW WHAT TO TALK ABOUT...
DON'T WORRY! JUST ACT NATURAL!
オロ
PANIC
オロ

WHY NOT INVITE YOUR CLASS-MATES TO HAVE LUNCH WITH YOU?
THAT'S WHAT SHE SUGGESTED, BUT...
IT'S NOT THAT EASY...

HEY!
WANT TO GO TO THAT ONE RESTAU-RANT FOR DINNER?
SURE. LET'S GO!
!

AH!
UM, CAN I GO WITH YOU?

SURE, WE DON'T MIND... BUT IT'S SUPER SPICY CURRY. IS THAT OKAY?
LET'S GO TOGETHER!
I'LL BE FINE!

I'M ALWAYS IN THE ROOM WHEN SHOUKO GETS HOME, SO I'LL SEND HER A MESSAGE SO SHE DOESN'T WORRY.
I'M GOING TO EAT WITH FRIENDS TONIGHT, SO I MAY BE HOME LATE.

ピロリン♪
PING!
ショーコ
GOT IT!

SHE DOESN'T... SEEM TO CARE...
しゅん
DROOP

BUT THIS IS MY FIRST TIME EATING WITH MY CLASS-MATES!
curry
THIS IS IT!
ドキ
BA-DUMP
ドキ
BA-DUMP
ドキ
BA-DUMP

THERE'S NO REASON FOR SHOUKO TO BE JEALOUS, AFTER ALL...
SERI, COME ON OVER!

I WAS SO SURPRISED WHEN YOU ASKED TO COME WITH, SERI!
ME TOO! I'M GLAD YOU DID.

SERI, YOU'RE SO BEAUTIFUL AND I WANTED TO GET TO KNOW YOU... YOU'RE LIKE A PROPER LADY!
THERE WERE A LOT OF RUMORS ABOUT YOU LAST YEAR.
AH! REALLY?!

THAT'S NOT TRUE!
I'VE HAD FAST FOOD BEFORE!
JUST ONCE, THOUGH...
AHAHA, I KNEW IT! A PROPER LADY!
THAT'S SO CUTE!

KER-CHAK
I'M HOME!
OH, WEL-COME HOME.

DID YOU HAVE FUN AT DINNER?
UM, YES. I ENJOYED MYSELF.
BUT THE CURRY WAS REALLY SPICY.

PAT
THAT'S GOOD.

WH-
WHY ARE YOU PATTING MY HEAD?
I'M JUST GLAD YOU HAD FUN!

I HAVE NO IDEA WHAT SHOUKO IS THINKING...

IT'S REALLY POURING DOWN...

YEAH.

WOOSHHH

UGH...
IT'S SO DARK. I CAN'T SEE ANYTHING...
SO SCARY!

KASUMI, CAN YOU GET THE FLASHLIGHT?
WHERE IS IT?

ON THE BOTTOM SHELF UNDER THE SINK.
UM...
UWAH!
ずるっ
SLIP

KATHUNK
OUCH...
SORRY. JUST DON'T MOVE.

SORRY...
SQUEEZE

I'M NOT SCARED WHEN WE'RE LIKE THIS, EVEN IN THE DARK!
WELL...
I'M SURE THE ELECTRICITY WILL BE BACK ON SOON.
AND THE LIGHTS WITH IT...

I CAN'T EVEN SEE YOUR FACE!
IF WE WEREN'T TALKING, YOU'D HAVE NO IDEA WHO I WAS!

NO...
I'D KNOW IT'S YOU BY YOUR SMELL!
すん
RUB
すん
RUB
WHAT ARE YOU, A DOG?

WE USE THE SAME SHAMPOO AND LAUNDRY DETERGENT...
SHOULDN'T WE SMELL THE SAME?

HMM...
I DON'T KNOW HOW TO DESCRIBE IT, BUT YOU SMELL SWEET.
THAT'S WHAT I THINK.

IS IT FROM ALL THE SNACKS YOU EAT?
I ATE CHOCO-LATE NOT TOO LONG AGO.
YOU PROBABLY JUST SMELL THAT.

I'D BE ABLE TO TELL IT'S YOU BY YOUR SQUISH-INESS.
HEY!
WHERE DO YOU THINK YOU'RE GROPING? CUT IT OUT!
むに
SQUEEZE
むに
SQUEEZE

BY THE WAY, ARE YOU NOT GOING TO GO TO CRAM SCHOOL?
IT'S TOO HOT TO CUDDLE...
OH, CRAM SCHOOL...

I'VE ALREADY MEMORIZED ALL THE MATH EQUATIONS WE'LL NEED THIS YEAR, SO I THINK I'M FINE!
TEE-HEE!
WOW...

THAT'S NICE...
YOU JUST MADE ALL THE STUDENTS IN JAPAN YOUR ENEMIES.

I DON'T CARE IF THE WORLD IS MY ENEMY AS LONG AS YOU'RE ON MY SIDE!
THE WORLD?

OH, BY THE WAY, I DECIDED ON MY MAJOR!
FINALLY.
OH, YEAH?

I'M THINKING OF MA-JORING IN PSYCHO-LOGY.
NOT THE CLINICAL KIND, THE SOCIAL KIND!

WOW...
THAT SOUNDS GOOD.
BUT WHY?

I DON'T UNDER-STAND PEOPLE VERY WELL...
SO I THOUGHT IT'D BE A USEFUL MAJOR!
TO MANIPU-LATE OTHERS.
TEE-HEE!
I SEE...
I GUESS I WON'T ASK ANYMORE...

FLICKER
OH...
THE LIGHTS ARE BACK ON.
UGH, SO BRIGHT!

PHEW.
I GUESS I'LL TAKE A BATH.
ME TOO!
MMPH...

KASUMI, WHAT ARE YOU GOING TO MAJOR IN?
TELL ME!
OH, UM...
ゴロゴロ
RUMBLE
ちゃぷ...
PLUNK

バチッ
CRACKLE
KA-BAM
WAH! THE LIGHTS ARE OUT AGAIN?
UH...
AND WE'RE STILL IN THE BATH!

I LOST MY CHANCE TO ASK ABOUT YOUR MAJOR!
WHOOSH
GRRR!

IT'S NOT LIKE I'M HIDING IT.
I'M THINKING ABOUT STUDYING NUTRITION.
CLICK

TO BE MORE SPECIFIC, FOOD NUTRITION IN THE LIFE ENVIRONMENT STUDIES DEPARTMENT.
FWAP
NUTRITION?
YEP.
FWAP

ALL YOU CAN THINK OF IS FOOD!
IT'S THE ONLY THING I'M INTERESTED IN...
I THINK IT SUITS YOU!
HEHE!
WHOOSH

LET'S DO OUR BEST DURING EXAMS!

YEAH.

Illustration gallery of Yukiko

Futaribeya
A ROOM FOR TWO

Bonus Chapter
"Fairytales for Two"

"Cinderella"

AH...
CRAP. I DON'T HAVE A DRESS OR SHOES TO WEAR TO THE BALL.
I GUESS I'LL JUST THROW SOMETHING TOGETHER.
ボロッ
RAGGED

バーン!
BANG
ABSO-LUTELY NOT!
OH.
MY STEP-SIS-TER?

I MADE A DRESS THAT WILL SUIT YOU, SO WEAR THIS INSTEAD!
THE MEA-SUREMENTS SHOULD BE PERFECT!
OH, THANKS.

THEY ENDED UP SKIPPING THE BALL AND ENJOYING TEA BY THEMSELVES.
まったり
LAID-BACK

"Little Red Riding Hood"

"Snow White"

"Hansel and Gretel"

TWO TWINS WERE THROWN OUT BY THEIR EVIL STEPMOTHER AND GOT LOST IN THE WOODS.
WE CAN'T GO HOME.
WAAAH!

OH, A HOUSE MADE OF CANDY!
ふら～っ
WAVER
NO WAY! THAT HOUSE LOOKS SUSPI-CIOUS!

トン
KNOCK
カン
KNOCK
I CAN MAKE A HOUSE, IF THAT'S WHAT YOU WANT!
IT EVEN HAS AIR CONDI-TIONING AND A HEATER!
トン
KNOCK
カン
KNOCK

I'LL BAKE YOU SWEETS EVERY DAY, TOO.
I'LL STAY HERE FOR-EVER!

"Rapunzel"

THERE'S NO WAY I CAN CLIMB THAT. I'M TAKING A NAP.
GOOD NIGHT.
すやあ…

ヒュン
TWIRL
ヒュン
TWIRL

す
WRAP
?!
ぽっ

TEE-HEE!
PLEASE COME IN!
ズルッ
SLIDE
YOU'RE CRAZY STRONG...

"Three Little Pigs"

THE HOMES MADE OF STRAW AND WOOD WERE BLOWN AWAY BY THE BIG, BAD WOLF.
SNICKER
にしし

OH? THIS BRICK HOUSE IS THE LAST ONE LEFT.

GUESS WHAT! ♡
I DEVEL-OPED A NEW KIND OF ANTI-WOLF DEFENSIVE EQUIPMENT! ♡

NO ONE WILL BE ABLE TO BOTHER US WITH THOSE AROUND! ♡
COOL.
EEK
SMILE
SMILE

"Sleeping Beauty"

LET'S SEE...
IN THE MANUAL IT SAYS, "KISS TO WAKE UP."
THAT SOUNDS EASY.
MANUAL

RUSTLE

?!
FWAP

I WAS JUST PRE-TENDING TO BE ASLEEP!
YOUR CITIZENS WERE REALLY WORRIED ABOUT YOU...
DUMMY.

“The Little Mermaid”

AFTER-WORD

HELLO! LONG TIME NO SEE. IT'S ME, YUKIKO.

THANK YOU VERY MUCH FOR READING THE THIRD VOLUME OF FUTARIBEYA.

MEOW
うにゃ

I'M SO GLAD I WAS ABLE TO PUBLISH A THIRD VOLUME.

EEK!

RECENTLY I'VE BEEN SLEEPING FOUR TIMES A DAY.

MY CAT WAKES ME UP TO GET FED.

IT'S SO HOT...

ONCE AGAIN, I COLLECTED QUESTIONS FROM READERS ON TWITTER.

aoiyukiko
PLEASE SEND ME QUESTIONS...

Q. IF YOU COULD ASSIGN COLORS TO EACH CHARACTER, WHAT COLORS WOULD YOU CHOOSE AND FOR WHOM?

ACTUALLY, THEME COLORS HAVE PRETTY MUCH BEEN DECIDED. SAKURAKO'S IS PINK.

BECAUSE SHE'S NAMED AFTER A CHERRY BLOSSOM!

KASUMI'S COLOR IS SKY BLUE.

BECAUSE HER NAME MEANS "MIST."

I HAVEN'T REALLY THOUGHT OF COLORS FOR THE OTHER CHARACTERS, THOUGH.

WHEN SAKURAKO WEARS LIGHT BLUE COLORS AND KASUMI WEARS PINK...

IT'S BECAUSE THEY'RE WEARING EACH OTHER'S CLOTHING.

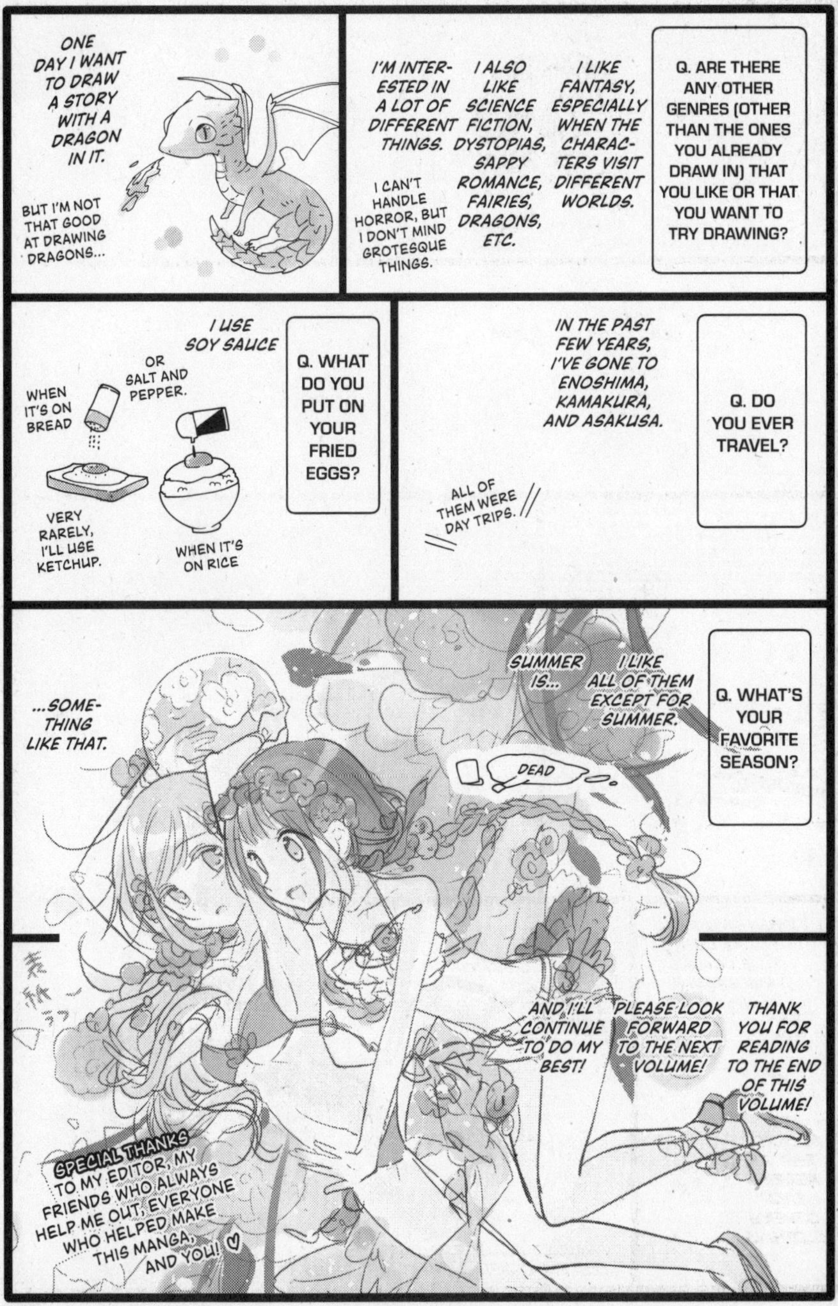

Q. ARE THERE ANY OTHER GENRES (OTHER THAN THE ONES YOU ALREADY DRAW IN) THAT YOU LIKE OR THAT YOU WANT TO TRY DRAWING?

I LIKE FANTASY, ESPECIALLY WHEN THE CHARACTERS VISIT DIFFERENT WORLDS.

I ALSO LIKE SCIENCE FICTION, DYSTOPIAS, SAPPY ROMANCE, FAIRIES, DRAGONS, ETC.

I'M INTERESTED IN A LOT OF DIFFERENT THINGS.

I CAN'T HANDLE HORROR, BUT I DON'T MIND GROTESQUE THINGS.

ONE DAY I WANT TO DRAW A STORY WITH A DRAGON IN IT.
BUT I'M NOT THAT GOOD AT DRAWING DRAGONS...

Q. DO YOU EVER TRAVEL?

IN THE PAST FEW YEARS, I'VE GONE TO ENOSHIMA, KAMAKURA, AND ASAKUSA.

ALL OF THEM WERE DAY TRIPS.

Q. WHAT DO YOU PUT ON YOUR FRIED EGGS?

I USE SOY SAUCE

OR SALT AND PEPPER.
WHEN IT'S ON BREAD
VERY RARELY, I'LL USE KETCHUP.
WHEN IT'S ON RICE

Q. WHAT'S YOUR FAVORITE SEASON?

I LIKE ALL OF THEM EXCEPT FOR SUMMER.

SUMMER IS...

DEAD

...SOMETHING LIKE THAT.

THANK YOU FOR READING TO THE END OF THIS VOLUME!

PLEASE LOOK FORWARD TO THE NEXT VOLUME!

AND I'LL CONTINUE TO DO MY BEST!

SPECIAL THANKS TO MY EDITOR, MY FRIENDS WHO ALWAYS HELP ME OUT, EVERYONE WHO HELPED MAKE THIS MANGA, AND YOU! ♡

Futaribeya
A ROOM FOR TWO

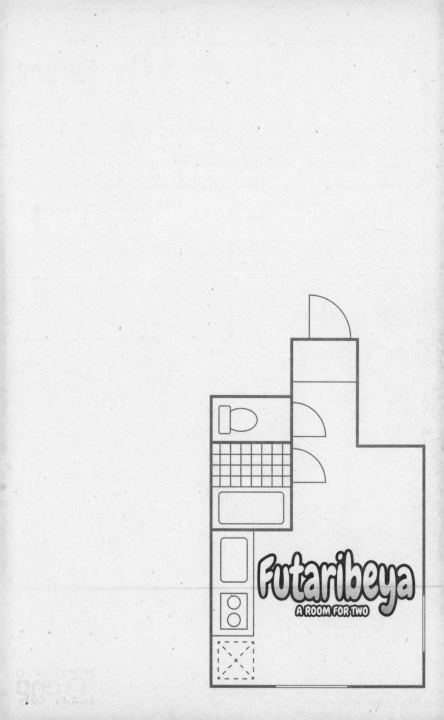

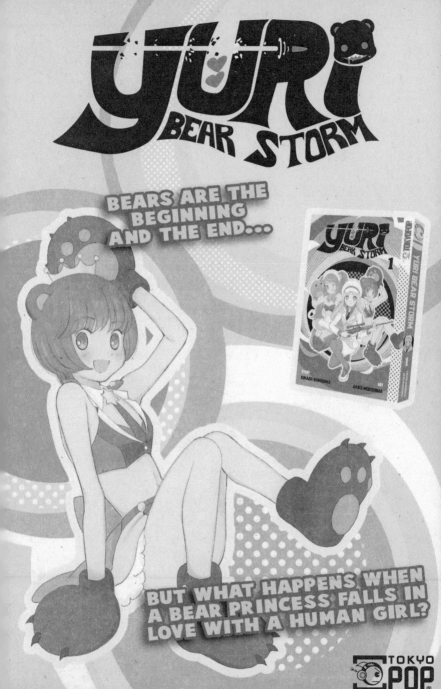

Sword Princess
AMALTEA

Join Morrey and his swimmingly cute pet Otta on his adventure to reverse his Midas-like powers and save his frozen brother. Mega-hit shonen manga from hot new European creator Nana Yaa!

TOKYOPOP
·PRESENTS·

UNDEAD MESSIAH
KAMO
PACT WITH THE SPIRIT WORLD

Ocean of Secrets

Sword Princess Amaltea
Natalia Batista
GOLDFISCH

TOKYO POP

TOKYOPOP®

Futaribeya Volume 3

Yukiko

Editor - Lena Atanassova
Marketing Associate - Kae Winters
Technology and Digital Media Assistant - Phillip Hong
Translator - Katie McLendon
Copy Editor - Massiel Gutierrez
QC - Keisuke Ariga
Graphic Designer - Phillip Hong
Retouching and Lettering - Vibrraant Publishing Studio
Editor-in-Chief & Publisher - Stu Levy

A  Manga

TOKYOPOP inc.
5200 W Century Blvd
Suite 705
Los Angeles, CA 90045 USA

E-mail: info@TOKYOPOP.com
Come visit us online at www.TOKYOPOP.com

www.facebook.com/TOKYOPOP
www.twitter.com/TOKYOPOP
www.pinterest.com/TOKYOPOP
www.instagram.com/TOKYOPOP

ISBN: 978-1-4278-6014-9

First TOKYOPOP Printing: February 2019

10 9 8 7 6 5 4 3 2 1

Printed in CANADA

STOP

THIS IS THE BACK OF THE BOOK!

How do you read manga-style? It's simple! Let's practice -- just start in the top right panel and follow the numbers below!

Crimson from *Kamo* / Fairy Cat from *Grimms Manga Tales*
Morrey from *Goldfisch* / Princess Ai from *Princess Ai*